Whitewater

WHITEWATER RACING

By Eric Evans and John Burton

A comprehensive guide to whitewater slalom and wildwater racing in canoes and kayaks

Contents

Dedication

At the 1979 World Whitewater Championships in Jonquiere, Quebec, Canada, American canoe and kayak racers assumed an unfamiliar stance in many classes, that of medal winners. It took 22 years for this to happen; while World Whitewater Championships have been held every two years since 1949, it wasn't until 1957 that a small contingent of Americans tested the waters of international competition.

From that start in Augsburg, West Germany, last-place finishes and DNF's in the ensuing years provided the foundation for respectable, middle-of-the-pack placings in the 1960's and 1970's, leading to the 1979 season when names like Lugbill, Hearn, Harrison and Fisher filled the top slots on the scoreboard.

Lest we forget, for every McCormick or Johnson competing at the top of his class, a Bill Prime or a Jo Knight had to battle to place 40th or 29th. For every Lugbill or Hearn showing the world classy moves on the water at Jonquiere, there were a lot of John Berrys, Dave Kurtzs, Bill Bickhams and Tom Southworths who paved the way by learning from the rest of the world. For every Harrison or Klein, women such as Jackie Paris and Barbara Wright had to survive an international race course before others could think of racing it.

To all those paddlers, coaches, race organizers and supporters of the sport in America who went before and took their lumps in international competition because someone had to start somewhere—this book is dedicated to you.

Whitewater Racing

1

Welcome to Racing

Do you enjoy doing well in your club's local races? Would you like to qualify for the Nationals? Have you dreamed of representing the country on the U.S. Team?

If you nodded your head vehemently or even slightly to any of these questions, then we would like to offer some advice: read this book! It is written for you, the person with an interest in racing kayaks or canoes in whitewater, or the person who would like to be more knowledgeable about the sport. Why not find out what you have suspected all along: you probably *can* race as well as the hot dogs who think they are so hot, and probably could have a clean run once in a while. The book is also intended for the already serious racer looking for tips on technique, training systems, or for inspiration. This book's ultimate goal is to help you do your best and have fun doing it, whether in a pool slalom or in the World Championships.

We believe firmly competition at levels less high-powered than the World Championships can be just as thrilling for those involved, and further believe it is not the medals and trophies that are the true rewards of success. We would like to borrow another phrase from another sport, then return to our realm. Vince Lombardi, incredibly successful pro football coach, has often and wrongly been accused of authoring the quote "Winning isn't everything, it's the only thing." Actually, and much more commendably, what he really said and believed was "Winning isn't everything, but the effort to win is." While reluctant to hang "everything" onto any one hook, we are in Vince's camp, and believe that the rewards to be gained from a serious, sincere, strenuous effort to excel in a sport, or any endeavor, are both obvious and subtle and can be incredibly satisfying. Further, our sport of whitewater racing has its own special attractions that enhance the quality of the experience to an extent attainable in only a very few other pursuits.

Simply stated, whitewater racing means going fast without making errors. As you are exposed to its intricacies, through lots of practice, hard training, and intellectual strain, it will seem to get more and more complicated. Then when you have the basics, when you have raced a lot, when you start making your own luck, it will be simple again. You will do well (and might win!) if you go fast without making mistakes, and by this time you will know how (or at least what it takes) to go fast and how not to hit the poles or miss your lines. And after your first breakthrough, when you are at the finish line breathing hard and you realize you have made very few mistakes, in fact you hit all the moves and might even have had a clean run if the myopic gate judges saw everything the way you did it (they didn't), it is then you will know the utter thrill of succeeding against a real challenge to yourself. We would like to emphasize again that the challenge can be significant at any level, and the rewards extremely satisfying.

It is possible to compete in and enjoy whitewater racing at several levels. People with some talent and desire do not stay beginners for very long, because one of two things happens after an initial stab at, say, slalom racing. If the paddler is not competitively inclined, but enjoys boating for its scenic, social, and relaxing attributes, as well as for the exercise, a whitewater slalom can be incredibly frustrating because it seems contrived and artificial. The heavy poles get in the way, cracking him in the nose occasionally, and require weird, unnatural strokes he is not used to doing. It is possible to realize no satis-

A beginning racer checks her score at the Frostbite Beginners Slalom held each fall in Vermont.

faction at all from a race, and to foresee none; this person's racing career is over, and he can get back to what he enjoys.

Alternatively, the guy who finishes last to the above paddler's second-to-last could react completely differently. He may be just as thrilled as can be at his small (and infrequent) successes on the course. He may finish the race saying, "Wow, that was fun! Next time I'll bet I can keep the penalties under 1,000." This is like Eric after completing his first marathon, in which he ran much too fast for 10 miles, only a little slower for the next 8, then limped in the last 8 in utter agony. Several hours later, in the same sentence in which he proclaimed bitterly that it was the most painful, stupid, idiotic thing he had ever done, he referred to how the next time, if he had any hope of breaking three hours, he would have to go out much slower.

Some of us have a competitive streak that will not allow us to continue doing an endeavor poorly. If we can't hit a golf ball straight, we will practice until we can. If we can't spell, we'll use the dictionary and think up memory systems to make us better at it. If we keep falling off 5.6 climbs, we'll keep at it until we get up, one way or another. This is one of the great appeals of slalom racing: definite, obvious, large-scale improvement is attainable relatively quickly. The basic moves to negotiate easy gates come pretty quickly, and the emotional difference between banging a pole which then swings all over the place, gets in the way again, and *looks* bad, and firing through a gate cleanly and smoothly in one or two strokes, is tremendous. The psychological rewards of improved performance come rapidly.

Thus it seems that good athletes, mildly competitive people, or those of us described above who abhor doing anything poorly, can use whitewater racing to make themselves feel good. The endeavor is enjoyable relatively quickly because there is positive feedback right from the start; a little practice, a little coaching, and the mysteries of yesterday are solved and become the building blocks for tomorrow.

Here it is important to note an often overlooked fact. Good racers make good river runners, and slalom training is an excellent enhancer of river-running ability. The reason is obvious, because the racer is required to be extremely precise and controlled at all times—he must make his boat go exactly where he wants. Slalom courses on big-water, rocky stretches of river leave no room for drifting, imprecision, or instability, and we have found that some of the strongest, most competent, most controlled river runners are also our top racers. Of course, there are many absolutely outstanding big-water river runners who have never been through a slalom gate, but that in no way belies the logic that great improvement in river running skills can be gained through slalom training.

Others become serious whitewater racers because the world of organized team sports can be closed

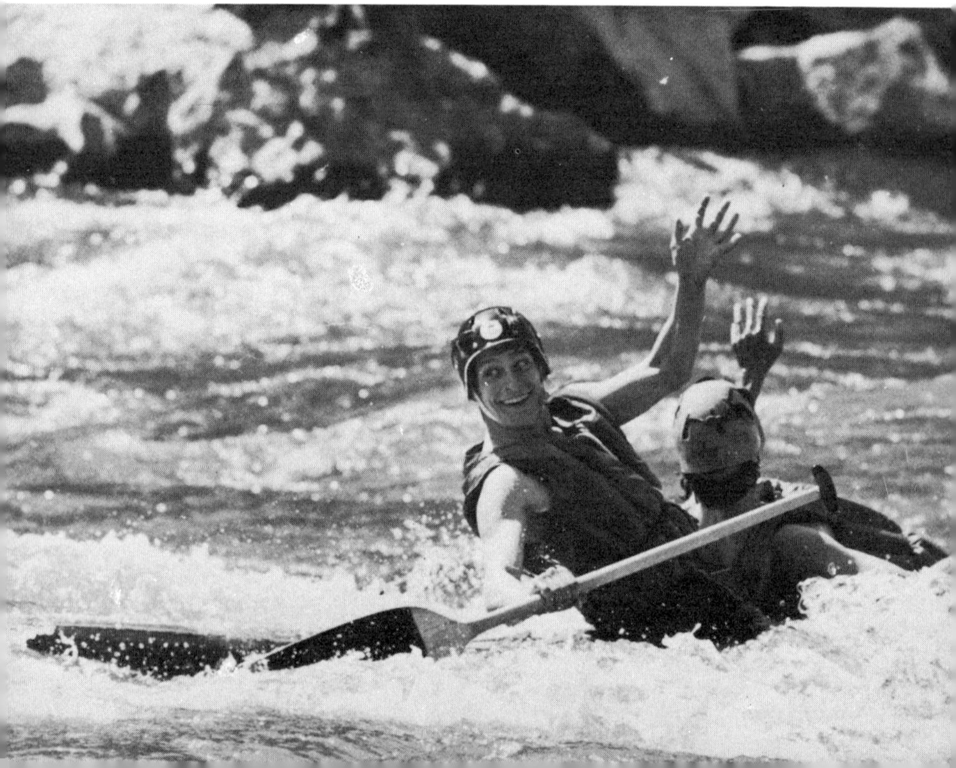

Noon on race day means checking your first run score.

to those who are not freaks of nature or who do not relish grinding elbows into others' stomachs. The average NFL lineman today might be 6′5″ tall, weigh 260 pounds, run the 40 in 4.7 seconds, bench press 400 pounds, and move like a dancer. An NBA basketball player is 6′9″, 240 pounds, quick as a cat, has a marvelous shooting touch, and hands the size of wastebaskets. The 5′9″, 160 pounder with some muscles in his upper body can be left out of these two sports at any level, from high school on up, especially if he isn't a "ferocious hitter" or doesn't like to "mix it up." But, that fellow can be the perfect size for kayak or canoe racing. Five-foot tall, 100 pound females have been World Champions in canoeing. Our sport is accessible to good athletes of no special physical dimensions or talents at all (look at Eric!). The upper body strength can be built, and the technique, quickness, and fitness can be learned in practice.

It seems that the one other sport in which many of our top paddlers have competed successfully is wrestling. Tom Southworth, Wick Walker, Les Bechdel, Jamie McEwan, and the Garvis brothers are successful paddlers who wrestled competitively for years, and there are others all around. The events are similar in that great

Being a good racer means you can have more fun playing in the big water. Photo by Jeff Leppo.

quickness, upper body strength, and real aggressiveness are required. The time span of competition is similar. Training for one is good for the other, and the mental toughness required in wrestling is very much needed in paddling.

We argue very strongly in the chapter on physical training that, in the off-season, competing in another sport can be very useful. Wrestling, gymnastics, and cross-country skiing are probably the best "off-season" sports for paddling, and if you are serious enough to plan your winter activities around what is good for your whitewater racing, then you have made the transition from a weekend warrior, a dabbler, to a serious competitor. You want to be as good as you can at racing, and that is what this book is about. The goal of excelling on the local or regional level is a big step up, for it cannot be achieved without a commitment to training, practice, and a search for knowledge. However, regardless of the results, in reacting to setbacks and successes it is still "not the triumph, but the struggle." It is important to keep the whole effort in perspective, to realize that your only competitor is yourself, your only real standard is your own last best effort. In our sport we don't hit the other guy, try to hurt him, elbow him to the outside of the turn, or embarrass him by running up the score. We are on the course by ourselves, concentrating totally on the natural and man-made obstacles in the way of the perfect run, looking only to ourselves for the resources to conquer this "opposition." If we succeed, what a thrill, and we receive the accolades of our friends as well! If we "fail," by not doing as well as we could, we can still take great pride and joy in the successes of our friends/competitors, we can still relish the bravery and display of remarkable competence of people striving for the same things we are.

This is not to say that we like tenth or even second place; the pursuit of excellence should never be satisfied, for very few of us are consistent winners at any level, much less World Champions. Therein lies another of the out-

Slalom racing sometimes can be a contact sport. Photo by Eve Eaton.

standing attractions of whitewater racing: there is always more to be learned, always higher goals to be achieved, always a new challenge. So, early in a racing career, it is important to establish high, but realistic and attainable goals, within the constraints of the commitment a person is willing to make. Do not expect to win a major kayak race after a month of beachcombing in Hawaii, or studying in the library; by the same token, don't be satisfied with fourth place in a race you should have won. Be analytical and critical without being a poor loser. Be disappointed in yourself to the extent it makes you improve your approach, your training habits, and your mental toughness.

The Regional Level

What does it take to excel on the regional level? It means a lot of practice in the gates, or, for wildwater, a lot of time in the race boat, on flatwater and whitewater. You must have talent, experience, conditioning and intelligence commensurate with the level you seek. Also, you must have a bit of luck, and hope the national team members don't decide to show up for the race you are trying to win. A factor to consider in a quest for local or regional excellence is there are few good races held in this country in any one season, much less on any given weekend. So don't expect to race against a bunch of chumps for the Eastern Championships, and don't expect to compete alone at *any* well-organized race on adequate water. Much of the U.S. Team will flock there.

The National Level

It is a curious fact that effort to excel beyond your own region will lead directly to the attempt to make the United States Team competing in the biennial World Championships. There are relatively few paddlers spread over a large number of classes: in 1977, more than one-tenth of the registered paddlers in the U.S. competed in the World

Championships! This means making the 1977 U.S. Team could have been a reasonable goal for any well-coordinated, serious athlete willing and able to make the necessary sacrifices.

At this level, unfortunately, a new, perhaps absolute, factor is introduced: innate talent. Per-Olaf Astrand, a physiology researcher, sums it up neatly: "Anyone interested in winning Olympic medals must choose his or her parents very carefully." We believe, however, that beneath the level of Olympic or World Champion, super inborn talent is not required (look at us!), because we know of so many average or even marginally skillful athletes who have succeeded dramatically, by any measure, in national and international competition. The ingredients making up their success are the old favorites—hard work, dedication, confidence and discipline. Therefore, do not shrink from setting high goals because you are not sure you possess the talent. If you can push yourself in practice, and keep plugging away at races over the years, there are almost no limits to what you can achieve.

The International Level

What awaits you at the end of the trail of grunting and groaning? Make no mistake about it, international competition is a gas. Competing on a national team, as a representative of your country, is a tremendous and special thrill. You will become well-known, you will get picked out of crowds (small crowds, of pigmies), you will get all kinds of ego massaging, but, more

Racer Mark Patlovich gets the count-down at the West River Slalom (Vt.).

importantly, you will feel the satisfaction of accomplishment, of excelling in your chosen field. We believe the triumph is in the struggle, in the hard workouts, in the early morning runs, in the weight workouts and in consistently pushing ourselves to work hard and improve.

The Commitment Required For High-Level Racing

Before you consider diving in to this melée and abandoning all other human pursuits, we would like to offer our impressions of what will be required of you—i.e., what you will require of yourself—in five key areas if you decide to realize your maximum potential.

Physical

You are setting your sights on the highest levels attainable in our sport, trying to compete with the best in the country and in the world. In the next five years, with better athletes coming into the sport, with America nearing the top internationally, the competition will only get stiffer, so you had better be prepared.

Physically, this means you must literally mold your body to serve the purpose. Raw power, the ability to explode through an upstream or across a raging current, is absolutely essential to success in whitewater. You must be able to pull your boat through the water with speed and control. Both the speed and the control require enormous upper body strength, and if you don't have it, you must build it. Strength building with resistance training (in the old days we just called it "weight lifting") is an essential part of every paddler's program of preparation, and some, obviously, need it more than others.

Of course, all the power in the world won't help a lick if you can't avoid the poles or the rocks; therefore, your second physical requirement is technique. Slalom and wildwater technique development require thousands of hours of work in the boat, with every coaching aid you can lay your hands on: videotape, movies, stop watches, mirrors in the pool, personal coaching and standard drills. Use every advantage or opportunity you can. If you don't, someone else will.

Building good technique requires accurate repetition of the correct skills—it is impossible to overemphasize the basics. After all, in a slalom you can only go through gates forward, reverse or upstream, and in a wildwater race, all you have to do is blow down the river. If only our sport were so simple! In fact, the best paddlers in the world are constantly working on and improving their technique, keeping ahead of the improving, hard workers who are giving chase.

The third physical ingredient that must be added is conditioning. You must be fit, able to paddle accurately at top speed at the end of the race as well as at the beginning and in the middle. In order to be fit for a five-minute slalom or a 25-minute wildwater, you must "pay your dues." You must put in the regular hours every day, month after month.

All in all, the physical commitment required to reach top-level competition is total. Your daily eating, sleeping and leisure habits must fit into your physical conditioning program. You must take care of and build your body. You must devote several hours of each day to the direct pursuit of your paddling goals, and before major races it will seem like you have only several hours each day for things other than training and race preparation.

Emotional

If you set your sights on a really difficult achievement, your whole being will become wrapped up in it—you will become, to some degree, a fanatic. Paddling will become the most important thing in the world to you, because your emotional well-being will depend on it to a large extent. This is healthy to a degree, because it can produce exceptional highs beyond anything most people ever experience, but you (we) must try to keep it in perspective.

It has been said "The quality of a man's life is in direct proportion to his commitment to excellence, regardless of his chosen field or endeavor." In our sport, no one achieves perfection, but there is no more satisfying endeavor than the realistic pursuit of the best you can do. Your emotional commitment must be such that success, a win in a big race or a leap above your expected place, causes a fabulous high, while a poor result (not, in any sense, a failure) will cause you anguish, anger and aggravation. Here is where perspective comes in—you must be able to rally quickly, to be gracious in defeat, and, above all, to use it constructively: Where did I go wrong? Why was I so tired by gate 20? How *could* I have been so lazy as not to fix my leaky boat? How can I prevent myself from being distracted by a penalty on an easy gate, thus causing me to hit others? How can I control my anger when I (or my C-2 partner) foul up a move? Here your emotional discipline will make you a better racer for having learned from a sub-par performance.

Mental

We believe the two keys in your mental approach must be toughness and discipline. These apply from the setting of your goals through planning and executing your training schedule to preparing for, competing in and analyzing your races. You will be called upon to concentrate harder than you ever thought possible, to shut out distractions and focus solely on the water, the boat and the required moves. Ignoring cheers or jeers from the crowd, wildly swinging gates, or poor weather requires unbreakable concentration. Slalom and wildwater racing, we have found, is an intellectual endeavor which can be done well (intelligently) or poorly (stupidly). Many otherwise fit and capable racers foul up a run by making stupid mistakes: turning the wrong way, coming too low out of an upstream, or not using the water. So often we have seen physically or technically inferior paddlers win races by being smart, avoiding errors and pouncing on opportunities.

"Whitewater intelligence" can be developed with experience. On the other hand, some paddlers, even at the highest levels, are cheating themselves and their teammates by not having the mental toughness and discipline to get the best out of themselves in workouts or in the races. It is so easy to "miscount" and do only eight instead of 10 repetitions of a drill. It is much more reasonable to save a little for later and not max out the 11th or 12th repetition on the bench press you know you could probably do if you really tried. Taking penalties on practice gates isn't all that crucial, since you will certainly be more careful in the race. Baloney—if you don't push yourself, or even allow yourself to be pushed, if you don't absolutely *hate* hitting slalom poles, you are shortchanging yourself. All the little extra efforts over the year, the entire discipline of your approach, will be worth it in the end because they *will* pay off, and when you win or really excel, the elation you will feel will make the little sacrifices seem absolutely trifling in comparison.

Social

With a serious commitment to racing your social life will change, at least during the paddling season, because your social circle will gradually shrink to your paddling mates and acquaintances at races. You will probably develop some intense friendships with people striving for the same goals you seek, while you may find the development of meaningful social contacts beyond the racing world more difficult. This will be due, partly, to a lack of time, but, more importantly, to the single-mindedness with which you will approach your sport.

Are the trade-offs worth it? We think so, because we value so highly the friendships of the people with whom we have raced and shared great experiences for so many years, and because they are, in general, an exceptional group of people.

Financial

We have come to the area of measurable commitment. You have chosen one of the last bastions of true amateurism. You will be able to feel noble as hell at not taking a nickel from anyone—because nobody is giving. This is not quite true, because many individuals and organizations have given generously to our U.S. Team Fund, but the total has never amounted to more than a small fraction of the team's expenses. Unless things change dramatically in the next few years (and there are folks working hard in that area now), you can count on paying 100% of your pre-team expenses and 90% of your on-the-team costs. After 1979, the World Championships will return to Europe, and your invitation to

69
73
67
71
95
56
59

be on the U.S. Team will have a $1,000 price tag hanging on it. Of course, that does not count money spent qualifying, equipment costs or lost wages. Racing will be a major drain on your finances, and you must plan for it.

Summary

So, welcome to whitewater racing, at whatever level! We hope this book will help each of you, because in it we are trying to deal with concepts, exercises and techniques that are applicable to all levels, and differ only in degree of intensity or precision with different goals. We hope it will be useful to you in your pursuit of excellence, however you define it.

The commitments required to reach the top are severe, but the friendships you make along the way last forever. Photo by Stowe Photo.

2

Slalom Technique

Of all the factors involved in whitewater slalom, technique is the most crucial. You may do well with poor equipment, while out of shape or with no sleep, but you will never get down the course in a decent manner with poor technique.

Technique is nothing more than the combination of paddle strokes and body/boat movements which you use to be in the right place at the right time under perfect control. There is no better feeling—to be on the fragile edge of control, a whisker away from disaster, for the duration of a 30-gate slalom. Technique is what makes whitewater slalom art instead of simply exercise. If it's a workout you want, there is plenty of snow to be shoveled or leaves to be raked. But for creativity and beauty it's hard to match what you personally can do on the empty stage of a slalom course—and your own special magic is possible only with good technique.

Keep in mind that technique refers to the basic moves needed for going fast and keeping the boat under control. Your style is your individual interpretation of technique, your personal portrayal of the basics.

The first part of this chapter will be seen through the eyes of the kayaker. In most instances, points of technique and gate negotiation are similar for both kayaks and canoes. However, we follow the kayak section with a thorough description of technique for both C-1's and C-2's. We conclude with several other training and racing tips, and an admiring look at the paddlers from the Washington, D.C., area who now dominate the sport.

Since readers of this racing guide are most likely beyond the beginner level with regard to basic fundamentals, topics presented here will assume a knowledge of the basic strokes and introductory lessons such as leaning downstream while ferrying, etc. The sections on both kayak and canoe technique would both normally begin with a detailed description of the forward stroke in each, but we have included these in the chapter on wildwater technique. Please refer to pages 103 and 107 for our forward stroke analyses.

Kayak Technique

Downstream Gates

There are usually 25 to 30 gates in a slalom course and none of them can be thought of separately. Each individual gate must be analyzed in terms of the gates preceding and following it. For example, your actions in gate three will be a result of the moves you make in gate two and the position you wish to be in for gate four.

Your object while on a slalom course is to paddle to the finish line in the shortest possible time while cleanly negotiating the gates. Thus, each combination of gates and each gate itself must be negotiated as close to full speed as possible while maintaining control. The more power strokes you can use, the better. Avoid correctional strokes, strokes for balance, and reverse strokes when going forward. Any stroke not propelling you to the finish line is hurting your time.

About half of all the slalom race gates you will run will be forward or "downstream" gates, so you must be able to do them correctly. The proper execution of a forward gate involves the approach, the negotiation, and the exit.

The Approach

a) Assume the proper angle for correct negotiation and maintenance of speed. The proper angle will be determined by your exit from the preceding gate, the position you wish to be in for the following gate, and how much of each end of the boat you can or desire to sneak.

b) Watch the poles and the water immediately preceding the gate and within the gate. You must concentrate; rest assured that glancing at the shore, your spray cover, or the gate number will not prepare you for going through the gate. It goes without saying that you must know exactly, without looking,

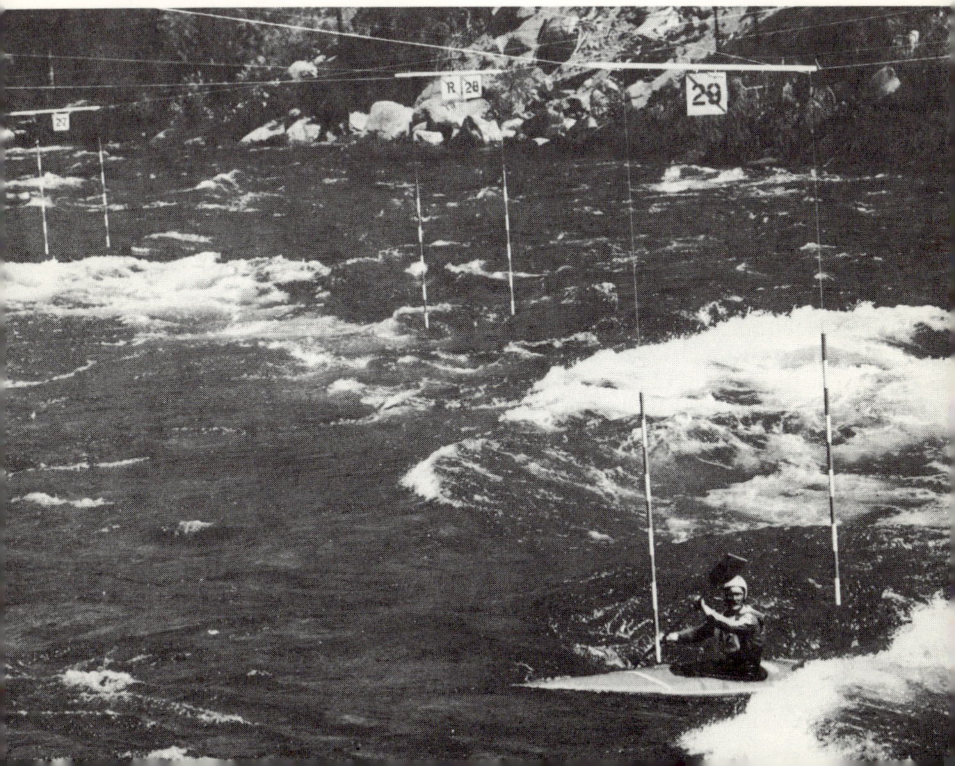

A good slalom racer thinks one or two gates ahead of the gate he is presently negotiating. Photo by Bob Woodward.

where the next gate is, because that is crucial to how you run this one.

c) Do not decrease your speed unless it is necessary to make a very tight or intricate turn during or immediately after the gate.

The Negotiation

a) Control of your boat is now critical. Make sure your paddle is either in the water or ready for instant deployment since you can only control your boat when your blade is in the water. In the old days of slalom, boaters would paddle up to the gate and then coast through with their paddles in the air so as not to touch the poles. It is far better to paddle through the gate without interrupting your stroke.

b) Raise your paddle shaft to as vertical a position as possible the instant you pass between the poles.

The Exit

a) Your body and paddle are through the gate, but you still have six feet of stern to clear the poles. Don't be too anxious for the next gate, and make sure the remainder of the boat makes it through cleanly. Stern touches are very common. (All three poles Eric touched during the 1972 Olympics were stern touches. He was too anxious about the next gate.)

b) Don't look back. With practice you should be able to "feel" where your stern is and how much of it remains in the gate. Looking back will only inform you whether you've cleared the gate—it won't *help* you in clearing it. Looking back also breaks your concentration for the next gate.

Offset Gates

Many of the turns in a slalom course should be done within the gates, to save time and to ensure the shortest possible line between gates. This is especially true with offset gates, two or more forward gates set across the current from each other. The incorrect way of negotiating such gates involves going straight through the first gate, turning afterward, paddling or maybe even ferrying to a spot above the next gate, turning above the gate, going straight through it, turning afterward, and so on, slowly and awkwardly down the course. Some offset sequences are so hard or are in such fast water that, if you do not know how to turn in the gates, you will have to back ferry between the gates or risk missing one or two of them—both disasters. Thus you must learn how to turn in a gate.

To figure out how to turn in the gate, refer to the first gate in the drawing (p. 17). As you approach the gate, you should aim for the outside pole, which in this case is the left, or red pole. If you make the mistake of aiming for the inside pole of the turn, you will find that you have absolutely no room in which to place your paddle and you will hit the inside pole with your right hand while attempting to turn.

As your bow approaches the outside pole you should do a sweep stroke on the left side followed very quickly by a Duffek stroke on the right. This Duffek should be planted before your body breaks the imaginary line between the poles (LBP). Hold the Duffek until the boat pivots and is aimed for gate two. You are now nearly halfway through the gate.

All of your forward speed has built up a great deal of momentum toward the outside pole. Now that your Duffek has turned the boat, you must do something with it to stop the momentum toward the red pole. You must draw and pull forward with the same blade that did the Duffek, actually making the Duffek-draw-pull combination look like one continuous stroke. The forward pull will send your body through the line between the poles and the draw will keep your stern from hitting the outside pole. In fact, you should leave the gate with the right side of the boat as near as possible to the inside (right) pole.

If you need to sink your stern under the outside pole, make your next stroke after the Duffek-draw-pull combination a forward sweep on the left. Try to keep the boat flat, lean back slightly, and concentrate fully on the next gate.

The principles discussed here apply to all sorts of gate combinations in a slalom and should be practiced on both sides. You will be surprised at how often the most difficult move in a slalom course involves an offset.

Reverse Gates

It is safe to say that you will have more trouble with reverse gates than with any other type of gate in slalom racing. This is because you will have to learn a whole new set of skills, strokes, and contortions in order to paddle precisely in and through gates while going backwards. You will find reverse gates harder to see, because you must twist your head and torso around quite severely, which is both uncomfortable and unnatural. You will have a tendency to take your eye off the gate more often than you should. Hopefully, we can inspire you and give you the tools with which to practice and perfect your reverse gate technique.

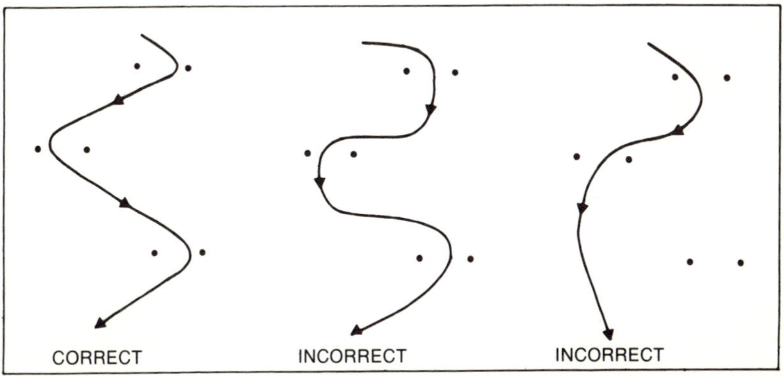

Don't hesitate to look over the section on reverse gates for C-1's, which necessarily goes into more detail on the complications of negotiating reverse gates in those boats. Here we present a generalized set of principles for handling reverse gates in a kayak.

The Approach

a) Continue paddling forward for as long as possible up to the gate. Paddling forward is faster than paddling backward, so you want to spend as little time going backward as possible. The better you become, the later in the approach you will be able to start your turn into the gate.

b) Turn crisply for the gate, using current differentials whenever possible—make the water work for you rather than against you. This means you will have to study the move from shore, watching other paddlers try it, so you can determine whether to turn left or right.

c) Sneak under one or both poles when you can and it is useful. Some reverse gates with high poles can be done completely broadside, but make absolutely sure you are just a bit reverse in the gate rather than a bit forward—the rules say that if it is close, the gate judge should give you the benefit of the doubt.

d) Do not turn high above the gate and drift, drift, drift down to the gate. If a high turn is necessary, paddle backward forcefully down to and through the gate.

e) While making your turn, never take your eyes off the gate.

The Negotiation

a) Watch the gate over one shoulder only. Eventually you will be able to see only one pole as you approach the gate, but you can still gauge your distance from the other pole from experience. Do not flop your head back and forth looking at one pole and then the other. The time it takes you to turn your head

Sneak the stern as you enter a reverse gate.

Look over one shoulder while negotiating a reverse gate.

is time enough for something to go wrong. In practice, make sure you become adept at looking over either shoulder.

b) As your body passes through the gate, quickly bring your paddle through the gate in a vertical position and down into the water immediately after the gate to control your boat. A common mistake is to hold your paddle in the air, trying to coax it between the poles, while your boat drifts into a pole.

The Exit

a) Be smart about leaving the gate. If the next gate is way downstream, you probably will not need to chance a risky sneak coming out, because you have time to turn completely after leaving the gate. On the other hand, if the course setter has given you a "gift" sneak by hanging the pole very high, by all means turn in the gate and sneak as much of your bow coming out as you can. That way you will spend the minimum amount of time going backward, which is one of your goals.

b) Some gate combinations are so tight that you do not want maximum speed through the gate. For instance, if there is an upstream gate waiting on the other side of the river only a few meters below the reverse gate, you will probably need to slow your momentum through the reverse so you can initiate the ferry while you are still in the gate. You may need to sneak out under one of the poles in order to catch the crucial wave that allows you to make the ferry quickly into the next upstream. That is when you will be happy you practiced sneaking into and out of reverse gates.

c) Try to angle your boat through the gate so that you already have a good start on the move you want to make after the gate. Once you begin to have very

Throw your weight forward to sneak the bow as you leave a reverse gate.

K-1W World Slalom Champion Cathy Hearn prepares to slide her bow under the near pole of a reverse gate. She has already snuck under the far pole with her stern. Photo by Will Summers.

precise boat control, you will rarely go straight through any reverse gate—you will be working on your next move while approaching and negotiating the gate.

Upstream Gates

Most slalom races are won or lost in the upstream gates. Overall aggressive paddling and hustle will save time during a race, but it will all go for naught if the upstream gates are poorly negotiated. The importance of upstream gates was demonstrated at the 1979 World Championships where 11 of the 30 gates were upstream!

Each upstream gate is different, demanding different moves. Some upstream gates are positioned in clean, distinct eddies which facilitate a crisp, easy turn into the gate. Others are placed partially or completely in the current and demand a wild flurry of strokes just to pull up in the eddy to the gate itself.

However, the majority of upstream gates may be done with two, three or four strokes. Before discussing the nuts and bolts of each of these three methods, a word

about the approach to an upstream gate is necessary.

The turn into and out of an upstream gate is the most crucial aspect of its negotiation. While on the one hand it is imperative you maintain your forward speed when approaching an upstream gate, it may be wise to ease up a bit during the last few forward strokes in the approach in order to get ready for a truly superb turn into the gate. Think of the phrase "Pause and Pounce," which refers to *pausing* for just a brief moment before making your turn and then *pouncing* on the turning stroke with all your strength. Wild, full-power forward strokes immediately before an upstream are likely to do more harm than good.

In the following discussion, "inside" pole refers to the pole nearest your body and the main current as you approach the gate.

The Two-Stroke Upstream

A "two-stroker" is usually done when the poles are high and both the main current and the eddy water are moving quickly (in opposite directions, of course).

The Approach

Since the current and the eddy are both moving quickly, in opposite directions, this will greatly facilitate your turn and allow you to approach the gate at a greater than 45-degree angle to the gate wire.

a) Sneak as much of your bow as possible under the inside pole as you enter.

b) Your Duffek stroke should begin before your body passes by the inside pole. In other words, it is done outside and upstream of the gate.

The Negotiation

a) After your Duffek, you should land in the gate with your body just about to go through the line between the poles.

b) With the eddy pushing your body through the line between the poles, all you do is reach through the gate and sweep on the opposite side from which you made your Duffek.

The Exit

a) The sweep will move you back into the main current and, coupled with a slight backward lean, will send your stern under the outside pole, and will push the boat out into the current.

The Three-Stroke Upstream

The "three-stroker" is one Eric learned in England while paddling with Peter Wilson and Alan Edge. It is most commonly used on flatwater or where the eddy is not moving.

Eric Evans makes the mistake of being just a bit forward, rather than reverse, at gate 12 Reverse in the 1979 World Championships. Photo by Doug Morriss.

The Approach

a) Paddle down to the gate at about a 45-degree angle to the gate wire.

b) Do not sneak under the inside pole.

c) In fact, your objective is to sneak six inches to a foot of your bow under the outside pole by placing your Duffek stroke just before your body passes by the inside pole; the Duffek is placed outside and upstream of the inside pole, though not as far upstream as in the two-stroker.

The first stroke of a three-stroke upstream is a Duffek. During the final part of the stroke, six inches of the bow will sneak under the pole nearest the dock.

Another view of the initial Duffek in a three-stroke upstream. Six inches of the boater's bow is now under the pole.

The Negotiation

a) As your bow sneaks under the outside pole (you may have to throw your weight forward in order to get under the pole) hang on the Duffek for a second to allow your boat to complete its turn and to bring your body almost up to the line between the poles.

The second stroke in a three-stroke upstream is a sweep stroke beyond the gate.

b) Reach through the gate for your second stroke, a sweep on the opposite side from the Duffek. Some paddlers move their hands up on their shafts to get more leverage for this sweep stroke.

The Exit

a) Your third stroke is a Duffek-draw on the opposite side from your last sweep stroke. This stroke completes the turn and starts your boat moving downstream. Since your body is extremely close to the inside pole as you start this last stroke, beware of hitting the inside pole with the top blade of your paddle when making this final stroke.

The final stroke in a three-stroke upstream is a Duffek-forward stroke.

The Four-Stroke Upstream

A four-stroker is used on flatwater or when the eddy water is moving in the same direction as the main current (in other words, not much of an eddy). This method can also be used when both poles are too low to allow sneaking.

The Approach

a) Do not sneak under the poles when approaching the gate.

b) Enter the eddy approximately two to three feet lower than you would for the Three-Stroke Upstream.

c) Your Duffek stroke should be made downstream of the inside pole.

d) You also want to land farther in the eddy than you would with the other methods.

e) With your Duffek, your bow will swing upstream, just missing the outside pole.

The first stroke in a four-stroke upstream is a Duffek. Note the poles hung just above the water.

The Negotiation

a) After the Duffek, your second stroke should be a strong forward stroke on the opposite side. This will keep your boat moving upstream and should also direct it at an angle back out into the main current.

b) Your third stroke is another forward stroke, planted just downstream of the inside pole. It should propel your body through the line between the poles. These last two forward strokes should not be timid, but should be deep, powerful, and full-length.

c) Your angle back into the main current as your body passes the line between the poles is extreme. In fact, your boat and body are very close to the inside pole.

Following the initial Duffek in a four-stroke upstream is a forward sweep which moves the boater up to the gate. The third stroke, shown here, is a forward stroke just before the body passes between the poles.

The Exit

a) The fourth and last stroke is a sweep on the outside, which sends your stern under the outside pole and moves your boat out into the main current.

Keep a couple of things in mind as you plan the exit from any upstream. First, watch out while leaning backward and upstream to send your stern under the outside pole that the main current doesn't catch your upstream edge and tip you over! Second, if the next gate is a tight reverse or is way across the river, you may want to reduce your angle of entry back into the main current.

The final stroke in a four-stroke upstream is a sweep after the body passes between the poles.

Pushing Off of Rocks

There are many instances in a slalom, especially in shallow, rocky streams, where a strong, well-timed push off a rock or other immovable object will provide a great forward thrust. The most common places to use this technique are as you come flying into an eddy near shore with too much momentum to stop, when the eddy is very shallow, or when there is a convenient rock above an upstream that can be used for a firm push out into the current. Don't hesitate to use these rocks when they are available; be careful, though, because they can often be quite slippery, causing the tip of your blade to slide off awkwardly.

A well-timed push off the rocks can increase your speed. Photo by Jeff Leppo.

Drills

The Two Gate Drill

For work on the basics, an excellent drill can be done with two gates on the same wire, 10–15 feet apart on flatwater. Simply paddle in circles through the two gates, turning as tightly as possible in each gate, so your path between the gates is as flat as possible.

This is an excellent drill for offset gates and for upstreams when done forward, and for reverse gates when done backward. As a suggestion, for starters, do 10 circuits of each exercise: forward clockwise, forward counterclockwise, reverse clockwise, reverse counterclockwise. Go as slowly as you need to at first to go clean, then pick up speed as you are able to handle it.

English Gate

At the end of this chapter is a very thorough description of how to do and use English Gates for training, with lots of useful general comments interspersed. Much of the real technical stroke and movement description there can be applied to the intelligent running of any slalom course. For work in a limited space of flatwater, the English Gate is hard to beat for completeness, symmetry, and difficulty. Any beginning kayaker would be well advised to master the English Gate as an integral part of his development as a complete slalomist.

C-1 Technique for Kayakers

Have you ever arrived at a gate and at the last instant found you had no room for your paddle and wished you could keep the blade in the water and slide it through the gate? Have you ever had your paddle blade "dive" or "slice" in the water just at the instant you needed support? Well, there is a way to refine your control of the blade when it is in the water. What you will have to do is pretend that you are a C-1 paddler.

This means using only one blade to control your boat. Drills for perfecting this technique are best done in a swimming pool or on flatwater. The first drill is to circle around a single slalom pole without hitting it. You should be using your inside hand (the hand controlling the lower blade which is in the water between your boat and the pole). You will find that you will have to do all sorts of crazy combination strokes to make the boat go in a circle around the pole. This will involve pulling, pushing, drawing, prying and combinations that do not have names. Remember, you mustn't cheat; the blade must never come out of the water. For C-1's this is a standard procedure, but is quite difficult for kayakers who must cope with a curved blade, a longer shaft and the lack of a "T" grip for the upper hand.

It is important to get the top hand out and over the bottom hand so that the paddle shaft is *at least* vertical. Another hint is that the top hand influences the bottom hand, so if you want to slide the bottom blade *forward* you must bring the top hand *back* toward your head.

After you have mastered going in circles around a single pole you should try to do the whole procedure in reverse. You might find this proves to be easier than going forward. The next step is to try to go in a straight line using only one blade in the water at all times. See if you can go around your pool or pond on your inside hand. Finally, try to do the two-gate drill we described earlier without taking your blade out of the water, in both forward and backward circuits.

C-1 Technique

Why would any fool willingly cram his legs into a boat by bending his knees, crush them on the bottom of the boat, and then sit on his heels? Usually, masochists of this type started out paddling some form of open canoe in their formative years, and the transition to decked-boat paddling was more natural with a C-1, where the strokes and leans were more familiar. Also, they wanted to be up higher in order to see better and not take every little wave directly in the face. (The *real* truth is they were terrified at the prospect of having to paddle on both sides, knowing the second blade would be a dangerous weapon in their hands. Of course, the response to the question of which type of boat is more difficult to paddle is usually "Half the paddle, twice the man.") And indeed, up until the last few years, the route to the top of the C-1 class was not nearly so crowded as in K-1, so it was not unusual for relative newcomers to make the U.S. Team in C-1. Today, that is no longer true, since we now boast at least six of the top 10 slalom C-1 paddlers in the world, and most of them are still very young.

The basic principles of good slalom technique apply to both canoes and kayaks because the objective is the same: the fastest possible time with the fewest penalties. C-1's have three advantages: the boats often spin faster than kayaks (partly because all the paddler's weight, including the legs, is concentrated over the pivot point of the hull); due to the higher position of the torso, the paddler can reach farther and can put more power than a kayaker into any one single stroke and, finally, this should allow him to do upstreams faster than the kayaker. Kayaks have the advantage of power and speed between gates and in long ferries, and therefore, are generally faster overall. However, our World Champion C-1's are now so good and so fast that on some courses they have beaten the kayaks in both time and total score. They do it by being incredibly aggressive, going for the absolute fastest route to and through every gate and, by being so sound in the fundamentals, they are usually clean.

While many of the basics are the same, paddling on only one side requires some special traits, some special stroke combinations, and even some special C-boat strokes, described below. For a complete description of the basic C-boat forward stroke, refer to page 107, in the chapter on wildwater racing.

Special C-Boat Strokes

C-boat paddlers use three strokes much more than kayakers: cross-bows, prys, and the compound back stroke, which includes the "far back" stroke.

Cross-bows

The cross-bows are a whole group of strokes which, when mastered, allow a "righty" C-1 paddler to do almost anything he wants with his paddle on the left side of the boat (his "off-side"), without changing the grip of his hands on the paddle. Keeping in mind the need for speed and accuracy, C-1's practice until, in all but the most difficult moves, they really have no off-side. Upstreams, spins and off-sets no longer need be considered "lefty" or "righty." On his off side, the top C-1 paddler can do cross-bow forward strokes, braces, draws, sweeps, underwater recovery to the next stroke—nearly anything. We've seen Jon Lugbill, current World Champion, take 10 strokes in a row on the right and negotiate two gates completely without taking his paddle out of the water on the right side of the boat—and he is a lefty!

Refer to the Two-Gate Drill described on page 25 and practice 10 circuits counterclockwise (if you are a righty) without taking your paddle out of the water on your cross-bow side. You must become proficient in these maneuvers to be

PCC
121
SUPERMA

Kent Ford uses a cross bow at the 1979 Nationals on the Savage River (Md.)

David Dauphine braces with a cross draw. Photo by Eve Eaton. (Next page).

31

The J-stroke, with the power face of the blade pushing out, is more efficient than the pry and does not slow the boat down as much. Photo by Jeff Leppo.

able to call on them instinctively when you need them in a race.

Pry Strokes

The pry strokes, which can be done anywhere along the side of the boat as far forward or aft as the paddle will reach, are very useful tools. However, in the effort to keep the boat straight between the gates, you must learn to use the J-stroke, rather than the slower stern pry. The more experienced you become, the more you will find yourself using the J-stroke in places you wouldn't have dreamed of using it earlier—it's a good habit to develop.

In big water, in unstable positions, or in making a sharp turn to your paddling side, the pry is often better than the J-stroke because it is more powerful and can be made into a brace very quickly. It also instantly becomes a reverse sweeping low brace as you push it out to the side. The only caution here is to beware of overusing it in turns into and out of upstreams because it is always slowing you down, when your objective in nearly every case is to carry as much speed as possible toward the next gate. For example, to turn out of an "on-side" upstream and head straight downstream for the next gate, you should transfer onto a Duffek or forward draw as quickly as possible, helping the current turn you as you accelerate toward the next gate. In this instance, hanging on to a reverse sweep or pry will not be as fast.

Since you don't have a blade on your off-side, you may need a *mid-*

The stern pry can be turned very quickly into a powerful reverse sweep or low brace.

ships pry to slide your boat to that side. For example, you (a righty) approach a forward gate too close to the green pole and you need to slide a few inches to the left.

The pry at your hip or thigh can very quickly give you the needed margin. Another common time when such a quick stroke is needed is when you are millimeters from the green pole in an upstream, side-slipping toward it, with your paddle deep in the water next to the pole: jam a quick pry in and you may miss the pole and be able to slide your blade through cleanly for the next stroke. Be careful, though, because the stroke will probably kill your forward momentum or stop you altogether, which has the double-barrelled impact of hurting your time and making penalties likely as you try to start from a dead stop within the gate. Always try to carry your speed through the gate.

The *bow pry* is a turning stroke which could be used to swing the bow down into a forward gate from a broadside position (for example, a righty, ferrying out from river left after an upstream, crosses the current and turns down into the next forward gate with a bow pry). It can also be used to initiate a forward to reverse turn to the off-side. For example, a righty, zooming into a left turn for a reverse, would plant a pry against the right gunwale three feet back of the bow to make the boat pivot to the left. The boat

The pry at the hip can hold the boat off the pole, while biting the tongue won't help much. Photo by Eve Eaton.

must be moving faster than the current in which the pry is planted or nothing will happen. If the water isn't deep enough, lots can happen: you will either snap your paddle as it catches on the bottom, mash your knuckles, or turn over so fast you will get whiplash. It takes courage to slam a pry into unknown waters, and good balance, but the results can be worth it.

Perhaps one of the most elegant and subtle strokes available to C-boaters is the *sliding pry.* To describe it we will use an example: a righty C-1 is in an upstream, facing directly up the river, too close to the green pole to be able to take a sweep stroke, which he needs to turn the boat out to the left into the current. Solution: a sliding pry, which looks like a forward stroke but has the blade turned at the plant so the inside edge is leading the pull back. This forces the shaft of the paddle against the side of the boat, and forces the boat (or really the front end of it) to the left as the blade is pulled aggressively back. This deliberate rubbing of the shaft along the seam line of the boat can be rough on the paddle, so make sure the boat is sanded smooth along the side and the paddle shaft is taped at the throat.

Another example: this time a righty is backing through a reverse gate, and as his body passes the line between the poles, the bow begins to swing onto the green pole. The next gate is a forward gate downstream on river right, with plenty of room to turn. If the good Lord is willin' and he gets lucky, the paddler can initiate a reverse sliding pry, from his right hip forward, with the inside edge of the paddle leading to the front, and push the boat backward and the bow to the left at the same time. This can be an awkward stroke, but if it is done right, look at the results: the boat

The bow pry on the upstream side turns the boat strongly downstream. Photo by Jeff Leppo.

The start of the forward sliding pry. Photo by Jeff Leppo.

has missed the green pole, cleared the gate, accelerated backwards and has started to turn toward the next gate. In addition, the paddle, at maximum forward reach, is ready to start a big forward sweep to turn the boat down to the left, toward the next gate. The kayaker could have accomplished this with a hard reverse sweep on the left, but that's too easy—the reverse sliding pry is a challenge!

One more example before we move on: let's say in the above example the gate following the reverse was an upstream on river right not very far downstream. Therefore, the paddler would want to stop going downstream and initiate a ferry across the river. In this case a forward sliding pry would push the bow and the paddle off the green pole, slow the boat down, and initiate the ferry to the next gate. Assuming the fast current pushes the boat through the reverse gate during the stroke, the paddler may wish to make the stroke continue all the way to the back and into a J-stroke, setting the proper angle for the ferry.

This completed reverse sliding pry has pushed the bow nearly all the way to the red pole, ready for a sneak. Photo by Jeff Leppo.

The Compound Back Stroke

This stroke has three parts: the far back, the reverse stroke and the reverse J. The far back is done with the same face of the blade as the forward stroke, only at the other end of the boat. This requires a severe twist of the torso, like sitting in the driver's seat, strapped in by a seat belt, and turning around to look out the back window. The shoulders and head must twist way around toward the stern, and the paddle must be planted right next to the gunwale, power face pulling toward the body, shaft vertical and top hand extended as far back as possible. Aside from getting all the kinks out of your lower back, this stroke, used in approaching reverse gates, allows fine control of the stern in the approach, can pull the boat powerfully backward, and forces the paddler to look at the gate. As we have mentioned several times, most penalties are taken on reverse gates, because the motions are unnatural, vision is difficult and most paddlers don't practice reverse gates enough. The far back stroke can be the key to a successful attack on this problem.

To practice the far back and the whole compound back stroke, go back to the Two-Gate drill mentioned earlier. Righties should be able to make 10 counterclockwise reverse circuits without taking the paddle out of the water; similarly, lefties clockwise. It is impossible to do too much of this kind of practice; if you think you've got it knocked, compare your time and penalties for 10 reverse circuits to those for 10 forward circuits, then get back to work.

We will describe a complete compound back stroke with a specific example, hoping the reader can generalize to the infinite variety of situations possible. The scene is this: a righty C-1 must do a three-gate combination of forward, reverse, forward, with gates 1 and 3, the forward gates, on river right, and gate 2 on river left, all in good current. What is a likely set of strokes for this series? The left turn above and into gate 2 will probably be initiated by a forward sweep out of gate 1, followed by a pry or cross-bow draw to complete the turn. Now comes the compound back stroke. The stern sliding into the gate can be pulled under the red pole and/or toward the outside of the gate with a far back stroke adjusted to be a bit of a stern draw. This should keep the boat turning and going backward, so that with the reach to the stern, the paddle is already through the gate! Continue the movement by quickly rotating the blade 180° into the start of a regular reverse stroke—this begins the second part of the compound back stroke. Push the blade toward the bow, forcing the boat through the gate, perhaps even making it a bit of a sliding pry to continue the turn by forcing the bow to the left.

Now, with maximum reach forward, the bow should ideally be swinging left underneath the red pole, a result the paddler can assure by adding the third part of the compound back, a reverse J. This just continues the sliding pry, but, if done violently, can slam the bow

The far back stroke pulls the stern under the red pole and then through the gate . . . Photo by Jeff Leppo.

. . . and when done correctly has the paddle through the gate very early. Photo by Jeff Leppo.

to the left. This would be especially crucial if the bow was still swinging to the right, toward the green pole. Now, depending on where gate 3 is, the move in gate 2 is completed by changing the pry into a forward sweep which, with the forward lean, forces the bow out of the gate, under the red pole, and toward gate 3. Notice several other things: looking over his right shoulder the whole time, the paddler never took his eye off gate 2—never! Also, the paddle never came out of the water while the boat was anywhere in the vicinity of gate 2, giving the paddler maximum boat control and the ability to avoid penalties. Finally, all the strokes described in the maneuver were useful, i.e., they kept the boat moving in the proper direction, were available to prevent penalties, and were in no way extraneous. It should always be so easy!

One final point on far backs and reverse gates in general: try to get your blade through the gate *early* each time. You will find yourself with many more options if you do so, and much less likely to hit the poles than if you get caught with your paddle "in jail," i.e., extended forward, caught between the pole and the side of the boat and with nowhere to go.

C-1 Upstreams

As with the kayaker, the canoeist must be hot in all three phases, the approach, the negotiation and the exit, to execute an upstream gate properly. The old saying is, "In slalom, penalties are made in reverse gates, time is lost in upstreams." Since C-1's, in theory, have the advantage in upstreams, let's see what that means.

Let's look at the ultimate "one stroker," the upstream gate in dead calm water a foot or two away from a strong eddy line. A high-speed approach, with the canoe aimed so

Photo by Jeff Leppo.

Photo by Jeff Leppo.

the bow misses the inside pole by millimeters, is controlled by planting the paddle above the gate during your approach. Here you must *lean* and *reach* forward, which cause the pivot point of the hull to move forward and allow the boat to pivot into the gate at a point only a few feet back from the bow. Your arm and shoulder strength is continuing to pull the boat through the gate as it turns upstream, always maintaining momentum *through* the gate. Now, as your reach is compressed by the boat's moving toward your plant, very quickly slide the paddle through the gate, in the water between the bottom of the pole and the side of the boat, into your next pull. If you want a super-tight turn down the river, guide the paddle out to the side as you slide it through, so your second stroke pulls you and the boat out and down into the current in a variation of a forward draw or Duffek. Be careful of your stern, and lean back if necessary to sneak it under the outside pole.

You have just nailed an up-

stream, left the crowd gasping, and gained a second or two on everyone! Wow!

Nowhere in the description was there a reference to on-side or off-side, left or right. The reason is obvious and may be startling: C-1 upstreams should be done the same way and at the same speed by lefties or righties, requiring that the paddler develop great ability and confidence in the cross-bow moves. Read the description of the C-1 upstream again, and try to visualize how the same gate would be done

These eight photos show both the on-side and off-side one stroke upstreams in a C-1 and make the point of how similar the negotiations of such gates are. Photos by Jeff Leppo.

by a lefty or righty in the same way.

You must be careful of your stern leaving the gate, trying to take advantage of the sinking stern on today's low volume racing boats. Here speed is rewarded: accelerating out of an upstream causes the stern to sink so the whole back of the boat is at or below water level. Done consistently, this means you should not have to worry about hitting upstreams as you leave. (If you must *ferry* out instead of turn down, you will not naturally sneak the stern, so you must be extra careful.)

Variations occur, of course. The "one-stroker-on-one-side" often gives way to the two-stroker: the lefty doing a right-hand upstream on his off-side does a powerful cross-draw as described above, then as his body passes between the poles brings his paddle back to his on-side for a strong forward stroke or sweep to complete the move. This also helps to sink the stern on the way out.

S-Turn Gates

Some of the most fun gates you will ever do (if you can do them well) are well-positioned "dive" upstream gates, where you come in from one side and exit the other in a smooth S-curve. Often the gate wire is positioned at an angle to "open the door" a bit and make it possible to really snake through. This kind of gate really separates the speed merchants from the plodders, since it can be done slowly in the usual style of doing upstreams, or it can be done with nearly no loss of speed by the high-risk move of flaming through the gate as fast as possible, barely missing both poles. The good C-1 paddlers will be very aggressive in a move like this, be it on-side or off-side, and will be strong enough to prevent the stern from swinging downstream in the approach. It is thrilling to watch.

A variation of this type of move is the S-turn required to negotiate two downstream gates on opposite sides of an eddy: the flatter the "S" the faster the sequence will be.

Two such combinations appeared at Jonquiere in 1979, one left to right, the other right to left. Once again, the strongest boaters were able to carve the straightest, fastest line between the two gates, flying across the top of the eddy while facing downstream the whole time! This required complete control in the approach, so that angle and speed and stroke combine in a flash of movement a whisker away from the poles. Many seconds were gained on the paddlers who had to do these moves with an eddy turn followed by a peel out.

Reverse Gates

Basic Principles

Before describing examples of the way C-1's should do various types of reverse gates, we offer here a set of basic principles of reverse gate negotiation you can use for reference in any situation. In no particular order:

1) Maintain speed. In approach-

ing, negotiating and exiting from any reverse gate, you should always plan to go as fast as circumstances will allow. In most cases, this means carrying as much boat speed through the gate as possible. Inexperienced racers can often be identified by the way they drift, rather than paddle, through reverse gates, hoping the current will not push them into the poles. Aggressive, confident, experienced racers will always drive hard to and through the gate, confident of their ability to control the boat very precisely, at high speed, backwards.

2) Turn into the gate late and turn out early. Another way of saying this is, try to spend as little time going backwards as possible—it is inherently slower. In modern, low-volume boats, this often means sneaking every bit of both ends of the boat under the poles!

3) Use the current. Often there are very slight current differentials near a reverse gate—either just above, below or to one side—that can help and even dictate the way you turn. Some reverse gates offer no choice as to which way to turn (for instance, after a ferry from an upstream), but often when you approach from directly upstream you have a choice of turning left or right. All other things being equal, let the current help you turn.

4) Know where you are going next. You must have a firm plan in mind as you approach every sequence of gates, so your moves in every gate are dictated by where you've been and where you are going. For instance, you would rarely turn right (bow right) after a reverse gate if the next gate is an upstream on river right—you'll be taking the long way! Similarly, if the next gate is an upstream on the same wire as your reverse, or only slightly downstream of it, you will not want to blow backwards at top speed through the reverse. You will want to be paddling forward in the gate to initiate the ferry over to the upstream.

5) Look at the gate! Never take your eyes off it! This is hard, say, for a lefty doing a left turn into a reverse gate, but the best lefties have learned to look over their right shoulders until they pass between the poles. This pretty much precludes doing a far back in the negotiation, but modern technique has the boater turning so late, i.e., one to two feet above the gate, that the entire reverse push through the gate can be provided by the reverse stroke or sweep that initiates the turn.

6) Take advantage of sneakable poles. The slalom rules now call for the poles to be hung no lower than 10 centimeters (about four inches) above the water, which in many cases works out to six or eight inches. Modern C-1's can go under such poles routinely, and with a little help can go under almost anything. In general, you should sneak any pole where the risk/reward trade-off is in your favor; if you *know* you can do it, go for it! Remember, sneaking does not have to be a violent movement, but usually should be a fluid part of the strokes that are most productive in a given situation. For instance, when you lean forward and do a hard forward sweep to leave a reverse gate, you

should be able to sneak almost the whole bow of the boat. Very high poles should allow you to blaze through the gate, concentrating on line and speed rather than cleanliness. Beware of mental lapses—you still have to get your body and paddle between the poles!

7) Practice! Reverse gates are very difficult, and deserve lots of practice time, under all circumstances. You must know exactly how your boat will react when you slam the stern under a pole at high speed. You must be familiar with the movements and sensations involved in twisting your neck nearly all the way around.

Examples

1) Gates 1, 2, and 3 are forward, reverse, forward, in a straight line down the center of the fast current, with plenty of distance between them, and no significant current differentials to help you turn either right or left. Here you have the maximum number of alternatives: trying to go as fast as possible through gate 2, you have four choices, left or right above the gate and left or right after the gate. For this discussion, we'll assume the paddler is a righty.

a) Left in, left out. This is a full 360-degree turn, and the sequence of strokes might be as follows:

Approach: The last forward stroke above the gate sends the bow to the left of the green pole, and in fact is more a sweep than a straight forward stroke. To complete the first 180 degrees of the turn, the next stroke is either a bow pry or a cross-bow draw; care must be taken here, because at this moment the stern is probably trying to sneak under the red pole, and a big forward body lean into the cross draw will probably cause the stern to rise up into the pole. Keep your

Dan Isbister takes advantage of high poles to go nearly sideways through a gate! Photo by Jeff Leppo.

eye on the gate over your right shoulder, even while doing the cross draw.

Negotiation: As the stern goes under the red pole, you should reach back for a far back stroke on the right to pull the stern through the gate and to the right (toward the river left shore). Try to reach through the gate with this stroke. Other possibilities would be to go from the pry or cross draw

right to a back stroke if you are deep into the gate, or, if you are *really* deep into the gate and moving fast, you would follow the pry or cross draw with a forward sweep to leave the gate by sweeping the bow under the red pole and out! That is known in the trade as a slam dunk.

Exit: Assuming you did not quite slam dunk this one, but needed a reverse stroke or even a far back and then a reverse stroke, you must leave the gate with as tight a turn to the next gate as possible. This means as soon as your momentum and paddle push have carried your body past the line between the poles, you should initiate a forward sweep to get the bow out under the red pole and downstream.

b) Right in, right out. This is a full 360-degree turn the other way, and while the strokes are simpler, you must concentrate on always looking at the gate, because it is easy to lose sight of the poles as you heave into a big reverse sweep to start the turn.

Approach: Your last stroke above the gate might be the classic canoeists' "C" stroke, which begins with a little draw to the bow, carves an arc with the blade under the hull, and finishes at the back with a slight J-stroke. This starts the boat turning to the right, and should be planned to end with the body centered above the gate and between the poles, the paddle poised to dig into a monster reverse sweep that will slam the stern down and downstream into the gate.

Negotiation: This can be a violent, very dramatic maneuver, be-

Left turn into the gate with a cross bow . . . Photo by Jeff Leppo.

. . . reach through the gate before completing the move with . . . Photo by Jeff Leppo.

cause it is so fast and actually a bit risky. The goal is a one-stroker, where the reverse sweep just above the gate is so powerful and so well timed and carries so much boat speed with it that it pushes the body through the gate before the paddle travels to the bow of the boat. Ideally, you are still looking at the gate over your left shoulder, as you did on the approach, and you have never had to take your eye off the red pole.

Exit: Now, as your body passes between the poles, you can switch your attention to the green pole as you are about to leave the gate by sneaking the bow under it with the continuation of your reverse sweep/stroke to the bow. This forces the bow down (you may need to lean forward to help the sneak) and at the same time pushes the whole boat toward gate 3, exactly as desired.

c) Left in, right out. Here the object is to turn the boat as little as

Use the powerful reverse stroke to propel you and your boat backward. Photo by Jeff Leppo.

. . . a left turn out with a forward sweep. Photo by Jeff Leppo.

possible, so you barely are legal as you pass under both poles simultaneously. This requires that the poles be high enough to sneak both at the same time without forward or backward leans. In this case the approach is similar to the full left turning 360, but the turn stops at little more than 90 degrees, i.e., nearly parallel to the gate line. Be careful—many top racers can attest to the risk of not turning quite far enough: a 50-point penalty. As the boat slides sideways under both poles, remember to keep it flat and "quiet." Smoothness and good balance are required here. Complete the move by drawing the bow downstream as you leave the gate.

If the poles are too low to sneak both at once, you will have to do more of a turn into the gate so you can sneak one end at a time. This may not mean a full 180-degree turn that has you facing upstream

The forward lean here was a little late. Photo by Jeff Leppo.

After the left turn above the gate, you see here the stern of the boat has been drawn under the red pole as the paddler reached through the gate early in the negotiation. Photo by Jeff Leppo.

The "draw to the stern" quickly becomes a hard reverse sweep to the bow to stuff the bow under the green pole. Photo by Jeff Leppo.

A slight backward lean will push the stern under the green pole . . . Photo by Jeff Leppo.

as you go through the gate, but requires at least that when you lean back to get the stern under the red pole the bow does not rise up under or into the green. Then, after the stern clears, you can lean forward after your body passes between the poles and, with a hard reverse sweep to the bow, drive it under the green and toward gate 3. This is a hard sequence of boat, paddle, and body movements to do smoothly, and often ends up looking awkward, and worse yet, with a 10 or even two 10-point penalties.

d) Right in, left out. Once again, with poles high enough, this move through gate 2 is a sideslip with the boat barely turned enough to be legal in the reverse gate. If the poles are low, the boat must be turned more, largely with the reverse sweep that initiates any right turn above the gate. Unlike the 360, however, in this move the turn is stopped as the stern makes it under the green pole by initiating a forward sweep at the bow. If the stern was really slammed deep into the water, you may have to pause a moment for it to resurface before trying to sneak the bow out under the red pole. The most common errors in this move are pushing the stern too deeply and not keeping the boat flat, so that balance becomes a problem or the lifted edge of the boat hits a pole.

Other Examples

2) Reverse after an on-side ferry. Here a righty is leaving an upstream on river right and after a high-speed ferry across a steep wave must stop the boat and back through the next gate. The problem is no easy stroke exists to stop the boat's ferry, start the boat going backwards, and sneak the stern under the red pole on the way in, all at the same time (which is ex-

. . . after which a forward lean will sneak the bow. Photo by Jeff Leppo.

actly what a reverse sweep does on a ferry from the other shore—How easy! How nice to be a switcher!). The solution is to use either a pry or a cross-draw to stop the ferry, and to be super-quick about it! If, with your ferry, you are barely making it above the reverse gate, you may well be able to lean back on your cross-draw and go through the gate on that one stroke—highly risky, but very fast. More likely, you will stop the ferry above the gate, then go to either a far back or a reverse stroke to push the boat through the gate.

The other way to stop the ferry and pull the boat into the gate is with a far back draw that pulls the stern into line with the bow relative to the current and into the gate at the same time. As often as not, however, this stroke is not powerful enough, and you will keep ferrying right into the green pole, or even beyond the gate! Rest assured this type of move is hard for all C-1's, so take heart and keep practicing.

3) Reverse after an off-side ferry. Referred to above, this move can be great fun because it just begs to be done daringly and very fast. Everything is working in your favor, assuming you make it to the gate in proper fashion—the reverse sweep you need to get through the gate also just happens to stop the ferry beautifully. Two pointers: be sure to keep looking at the gate—if you have to switch to your on-side shoulder, do it quickly. Try to resist the tendency to go to a far back to get into the gate; it is much faster and actually cleaner to slam through the gate on your reverse sweep. Go for it!

4) Reverse followed by a tight upstream. With an upstream on the same wire or just downstream of a reverse, you must plan to make the *combination* as fast as possible, not necessarily the reverse gate alone. If you fire through the reverse, you will get to the upstream low and take lots of extra time to get through it. So, approach the reverse briskly, but be aware you must slow the boat down as you go through it. This is one place where the really strong, fit paddler can gain time, precisely because he is strong enough to maintain his speed into the gate and then stop the boat in it. The weaker paddler must slow the boat down earlier, thus losing valuable seconds.

Offset Gates

Combinations of two, three, or even four forward gates in a row can be very difficult in fast water, because there is so little room for mistakes! Course designers seem to take perverse delight in setting such gates as far across the river from each other as possible, making them look outrageously difficult. In fact, they often are, but usually careful study of the currents, proper boat speed and angle, well-timed strokes, and lots of hard paddling can get you through.

Return for a minute to our description of how to do offsets in a kayak on page 16, and realize that the boat movement and angle principles are the same for all types of boats. The fastest line through the sequence requires you to turn above or in a gate in preparation for the next one.

Example 1

Gates 1, 2, and 3 are all forward with 1 and 3 on river right and 2 way over on river left. The current is fast, and if you lose control going for gate 2 you will hit it, maybe fifty it, and probably miss gate 3. Pray for some luck, and try to do the sequence as follows. You are a righty.

Your speed and angle of approach to gate 1 may well determine whether you make gate 3, not to mention gate 2! You would like to be pointing to the left as you go through 1, if possible sneaking lots of your bow under the red pole. You should take a giant forward stroke or forward sweep as your body passes between the poles, which accelerates your body and boat through the gate, toward gate 2, and sinks the stern under the green pole (you may need to lean back a bit here). If the bow of your boat cannot go under the red pole in 1, it should slide by within an inch.

You must hustle to gate 2! Your paddle is on the downstream side of the boat and the current is pushing you downstream, so you have to really hammer it to get over to gate 2 in time. (Beware of shallow water here—a paddle breaker for sure.) Consider switching to the left, or doing aggressive cross-bow forward strokes. You are aiming for a point *above* gate 2, so that you can turn toward gate 3 before or as you get to gate 2. In either case, your boat will be doing some or all of the turn toward 3 while in gate 2. Thus, 2 is very difficult to do clean. It is possible a reverse sweep on the right just above the green pole will be the correct stroke if you need to turn sharply, stop your flight to the left shore, sneak your bow under the red pole, or all three. Because this slows you down, though, it would usually be preferable to do this gate on a Duffek or draw stroke of some kind. While above or in gate 2, you must work hard to line up properly for gate 3. Your hope, as your body crosses the line between the poles, is to be able to slice your blade forward in the water, millimeters away from the bottom of the pole, to reach for the next stroke, a draw/forward combination pulling you to gate 3. If you lean back as you exit, you may even sneak your stern under the red!

Going for 3, your paddle is on the upstream side of the boat, lethal tip catching is no longer a worry, and you should be able to power over to 3. Care must be taken here, however, not to bury the upstream edge of the boat and lose your balance, causing a low brace and a shrug at gate 3 as you are blown by it. You must lean away from your forward strokes between 2 and 3 to prevent catching a "rail," or gunwale.

Assuming gate 4 is over on river left (the diabolical course designer will see to it), we can describe the proper negotiation of gate 3 as an offset and have covered all situations—lefties just substitute sides in the descriptions to figure your strokes. In the approach from 2 to 3, you are again striving to be able to turn above 3 for 4. The most likely "last" stroke to turn you into 3 and toward 4 is a violent cross-bow draw—look what it can accomplish: if necessary, you can submerge the bow of your boat under the green (outside) pole as you lean onto the cross-draw. It slows you down, perhaps better setting up the path to 4 (but perhaps slowing you down too much—be careful). It puts your paddle on the inside of the turn, and if you are deft enough, you can go all the way through 3 on your cross side. You would reach through the gate, just missing the bottom of the red pole with the knuckles of your right hand, and go immediately into a cross-bow forward stroke. This will help prevent your body from drifting into the green pole, and can pull you toward your next objective, gate 4. You may well keep going on your cross side if necessary, but it is more likely that somewhere in there you will want to snap your paddle quickly over the bow deck and dig in with a strong forward stroke or sweep. This will help sneak your stern under the green, especially if you lean back.

Sound easy? It's not, and requires lots of practice. Even on flatwater you can practice most of the elements of difficult offsets by really working on in-the-gate turns. Paddle control and stroke timing must be practiced over and over. Quickness and strength really help here, but well-done offsets will always demonstrate excellent technique.

Special C-1 Problems

Off-side Ferries

Beginning canoeists have the hardest time with one particular aspect of their chosen craft: it keeps wanting to turn away from a forward stroke. The most deadly situation that demonstrates this tendency finds the righty C-1 stopped dead in a river-left eddy, with a tough ferry waiting and no speed to enter the current; every forward stroke, it seems, must be immediately followed by a J or pry which kills the momentum, yet you know that as soon as you put your bow out across the eddy line you had better be going fast or you will kiss the ferry goodbye. What to do?

Switch! Your problems are over, because with your paddle now on the downstream side of the ferry you can prevent the bow from being blown downstream after you cross the eddy line. But that's too easy (or out of the question) you say, because it doesn't respond to the problem of the one-sided boater who has no intention of zooming onto that hairy wave on his bad side. Is there any way to do it without switching?

As a matter of fact there are three!

1) Try a couple of cross-bow forward strokes to get you going; if you are cocky enough, you could even go out into the ferry on your off-side, but that takes years of practice. One or two strong cross-bow forward strokes may be enough to allow you to move quickly into J-strokes that will propel you out across the eddy line at the proper angle.

2) You *can* do it with forward strokes on the right, if you really reach far forward and take very long strokes with the blade of your paddle as far under the hull as possible. These are aggressive "C" strokes, done with the blade as close under the center line of the boat as possible.

3) Use a good paddle plant off a rock or the shore. Don't hesitate to reach back and jam your paddle into whatever firm object is available; a strong push-off will start you upstream and not turn the bow to the left. Then as your whole boat crosses the eddy line almost at once, you can attack the ferry with hard forward strokes, leaning downstream all the while. This is a tough move, made more difficult because your balance is so precarious.

Steering

Once again, we would like to emphasize the importance of developing the habit of using the J-stroke to steer rather than the pry whenever possible. In going forward, or in paddling hard upstream in difficult off-side ferries, you will have better speed if you can correct the turning tendency of your C-1 with the J. It is inherently faster.

C-2 Slalom Technique

The name of the game in C-2 slalom these days is "Gemini," or more broadly, "close cockpit boats." Tried unsuccessfully many years ago, but stymied by the old rule which required the ends of a C-boat to be higher than the middle, close cockpit boats (with both paddlers in the middle of the boat, cockpit rims 18–25″ apart and offset to the paddlers' sides) are now here to stay. The absence of the old rule is crucial in one aspect: it allows huge amounts of volume to be taken *out* of the ends of the boat, and today's C-2's have only a fraction of the total volume they used to have.

What does this mean? It means the boats can be made much lighter, because there is much less of them. The boat will turn faster, because the weight is closer to the pivot point (similar to the way a spinning figure skater with arms out to the side spins faster as the

The Gemini in the 1977 World Championships. Photo by Eve Eaton.

In the old days, boats were bigger, and the paddlers were closer to the ends.

arms are brought into the torso); also, the ends of the boat can sneak easily. It means modern C-2 paddling is very much like C-1 paddling with no off-side. It means the boats are much more stable upright yet easier to roll after disaster has struck; finally, it means enders are more fun!

We will examine each of these points and discuss their implications.

(1) Weight: Though still 4.58 meters long (15 feet) and 80 cm wide, modern racing C-2's have weighed in, fully outfitted, at little more than 20 pounds! There is simply less boat there than before, largely because fore and aft of the cockpits the ends taper very quickly to nothing. The boats look very much like C-1's and kayaks, and because they are so light and so small in the ends, they are now paddled very similarly.

(2) With the weight concentrated in the center, with paddlers still able to reach nearly to the ends, and with so little cross-sectional area in the ends to drag through the turns, the modern close-cockpit boats turn much more easily than end-hole boats.

Combine this with (3) the ability to sneak, and the boats can do much tighter maneuvers than the old boats. What it boils down to, especially with the new rule placing

Center-cockpit C-2's seem more stable than the end-hole variety. Photo by Eve Eaton. (Next page)

407

152
N.O.C.

the poles 10 cm or more off the water, is that the whole boat does not need to go through the gate. This applies in upstreams, reverses, offsets, and nearly any move requiring some turning in the gate. We find ourselves doing extremely tight combinations in practice which will not likely be repeated in races, but whose teaching value is undeniable: if we can learn to do turns crisply and quickly and in shorter distances, it still means we will spend less time sideways and backwards, more time going forward toward the objective, and have more time to be careful, to avoid penalties.

(4) Paddling center cockpit boats is so much like paddling C-1 that teams of top C-1 paddlers don't seem to need to practice together in the C-2. It can be argued the two best U.S. slalom C-2's currently are Jon Lugbill/Bob Robison and David Hearn/Ron Lugbill. They never train together, yet they usually win the races they enter. Since these are usually only the important races, it is quite frustrating for the long-suffering C-2 partnerships who beat their brains working on teamwork. Jon, Bob, David, and Ron also happened to place 1st, 3rd, 2nd, and 5th in the 1979 World Championships in slalom C-1. They have a good bit of talent on which to fall back when they dust off the old C-2 and hop in at the start line.

A Gemini bow man sits about as far from his bow as he does in his C-1, and, similarly sits the stern man relative to his end of the boat. This causes the negotiation of the gates, especially upstreams, to be remarkably similar to the way it is done in C-1. The angles in and out, the clearances, the width of the boat at the paddler's seat, are all similar to the C-1. What is *better* is that there is really no off-side for either paddler, since he has his partner's strokes and braces ready to take up any slack.

A major difference paddlers will discover in going from an end-hole boat to a center-cockpit design, is that the timing of forward and backward leans now becomes crucial, because sneaking is now crucial. In the old tubs we used to paddle, sneaking was out of the question because the ends of the boat were so big.

(5) Partly because the cockpits are offset to the paddlers' paddling sides, the inertia of the boat in resisting rolls is greater. Also, it seems that sitting closer together the paddlers can communicate better, can feel each other's movements in the boat better. (Don't ask us to explain that one!) In any case, the boats are much more stable, and definitely easier to roll. It seems the latter fact is true because in the center of the boat, each paddler's roll is stronger, works better against the whole boat, than in the ends.

(6) Most teams have found, above all else, the center cockpit boats are fun to paddle. Their confidence level goes way up, because they are more stable in the boat and have better results in roll attempts. This makes playing more fun, and big-water playing becomes

---

Hope for deep water when you try a C-2 ender. Photo by Jeff Leppo.

a gas. And, best of all, the broad expanse of flat deck in front of the bow man just invites enders, which when done in front of an appreciative crowd and/or a movie camera, are the ultimate. Until you have experienced an Airborne, Waving, Pirouetting, Slam Dunking Ender for a crowd, you have not experienced everything the sport has to offer.

The C-2 Partnership

Before talking about technique, let's talk about partnerships. As the word implies, C-2 partners are in this thing together, and must strive always to do what is best for the partnership. This means subjugating personal goals to those of the team, and it means being very honest with yourself and your partner about what your *true* goals are.

Ask yourself these questions:

Do you really like the guy with whom you are proposing to spend endless hours in a cramped boat, working on basics until you are sick of it?

Do you believe your partner carries half the load?

Do you believe your partner makes more than his share of mistakes?

Do you think he is out to show you up?

Does he train as hard as you do?

Does he care about racing as much as you do?

What it all boils down to, is you both have to have fun or it is not worth it. It must be a set of enjoyable experiences: planning, training, driving to races, sharing both the ups and downs. The concept of blame for mistakes should never even come up; each paddler must admit to his own weaknesses and mistakes, and be infinitely under-

The C-2 partnership has to be fun and rewarding for both parties.

standing of his partner's. They must try to help each other at every opportunity, and they must always be fighting for the same thing: the best possible results for the partnership, and to see that the other guy has a good, fun experience.

The beauty and appeal of C-2 lies in the teamwork, the precision, the overcoming of complications, the understanding and the communication. In the end, after all the work, the frustrations, the dependency and the pushing, success will produce a greater high than in the individual classes. You will feel not only the wonderful sense of accomplishment at your own achievement, but will rightfully revel in the good spirits of your partner, because you had a hand in his accomplishment and joy. There is no better feeling in sport.

C-2 Timing and Teamwork

Beyond the usual attributes of strength, quickness, fitness, and talent, the keys to successful C-2 slalom racing are timing and teamwork. These two factors will be continually emphasized as we discuss ways of doing upstreams, reverses and offsets.

Upstreams

There are two methods of doing upstreams in center cockpit boats, differentiated by the handling of the bow and the leans in the start of the turn into the gate.

We'll call the first method the "C-1 technique," since it basically resembles the way singles boaters do it. The bow man must guide the high-speed approach to the gate so the bow knifes around the inside pole and just misses hitting the outside pole as it swings in. He must pull the bow forward and up into the gate, doing his best to maintain boat speed all the way through. As the stern man helps him to drive up through the gate, he must make sure to get his paddle through quickly, so he doesn't get caught right on the pole with his paddle still downstream of it, with no space to get his hand and the paddle shaft through.

Off-side moves for the bow man can be very awkward because he often cannot get the cross-draw out of the water without hitting the inside pole. Perhaps in this case the team is trying too tight a turn, and should turn into the gate a little lower so it can stroke smoothly and together all the way through.

The stern man's job is to provide push into the gate, whether it is a right or a left turn in. When his paddle is on the inside of the turn, he should try to help carve the turn with perhaps a slight reverse sweep followed by a Duffek, which will help stop the boat from sideslipping to the outside and will keep the momentum going upstream. Both paddlers must be careful of pulling out of the gate too soon, thus jamming the stern man on the inside pole.

The second method, which we are calling the "C-2 technique," has been invented to take advantage of the sneakability of the bow of a Gemini when both paddlers lean forward and lean the boat into the

198
N.O.C.

32
31

This boat is in danger of cutting out of the upstream too soon, jamming the stern man on the inside pole. Photo by Jeff Leppo.

turn. The basic difference is, on the approach, the boat is driven further across the gate before turning up into it, so much so that the front must be snuck under the outside pole (much like the three-stroke upstream in a kayak). It is done this way both on-side and off-side. It is risky and the timing must be perfect, but if it works the reward is terrific: upon completing the bow sneak, the bow man finds himself much deeper into the gate, so he has much less difficulty getting his paddle through—it already is!

For the off-side turn, the move is as follows: with a good head of steam across the current toward the gate, the paddlers drive across the eddy line and the bow man plants a big cross-draw *in* the gate, reaching up between the poles if he can. The stern man does a reverse as hard as he needs to, and, simultaneously, they both lean forward and dip the upstream gunwale. The nose slides under the outside pole, pops up in the gate, and the bow man is already through it! The stern man's next stroke is forward, planted right next to the inside pole, while the bow man is yanking him up through on a forward stroke

With a powerful drive upstream, the bow of this boat will sneak in under the outside pole and the bow man will find himself in the gate. Photo by Eve Eaton.

after the cross-draw. It is really slick when it works, but the timing has to be perfect.

It is a little harder to do this on the bow man's on-side, because the available strokes simply are not as powerful for sneaking—it is harder to get the bow under the outside pole with a draw. It can be done, but it takes practice and patience. We believe, to be competitive in the future, C-2's must have this trick up their sleeves, because it is so fast when it is done right.

A Note on Rhythm and Timing

It is important in upstreams and in all C-2 paddling for the partners to make every effort to paddle together. There should be a rhythm, a cadence, set by the bow man that becomes natural for both. The bow man, who cannot see but can feel what his partner is doing, must consciously time his strokes so his partner has the easiest possible time matching him. If he knows the stern needs a big pry that will take a few extra fractions of a second, he must slow the recovery from his last stroke to his next so his partner can catch up.

In general it makes sense, if there is a big weight and reach difference between the two paddlers, for the bigger person to be in the bow. His naturally longer and slower stroke will allow the stern man to steer and keep up with the pace; if the seats were reversed, the bigger man would have a doubly hard time as he needed to put in his J's and prys for steering.

Reverse Gates

Off-side Reverse Spins

Good teams work out signals and body language to anticipate each other's strokes. For example, in approaching a reverse gate for which they have planned an off-side turn (that is, turning the bow away from the bow man's paddling side), a C-2 team must try to do its strokes together. The first turning stroke for each of them is a pry (or perhaps a cross-draw for the bow man), but there is a problem: the bow man's pry is at the front, at the place where he normally starts his stroke. The stern man's pry or reverse sweep is initiated at the back, at the place where he normally ends his stroke. Without preplanning and some alteration of pace, they will mistime their strokes by half a beat as the bow is late starting the move. How do they hit the first stroke together?

A good method is to have the bow man make his last stroke prior to the pry or cross-draw be a short, abbreviated sweep, after which he quickly slams the paddle into his turning stroke. This little sweep not only starts the turn, but warns the stern man that the actual turn is starting. It is an easy and natural movement for the stern man to finish his normal forward stroke by going immediately into the necessary pry or reverse sweep. With practice and a real effort at consistency, this communication becomes automatic.

Let's continue the example, and observe the well-timed C-2 team continue the negotiation of the reverse gate. Ideally, they would like to stroke together every time, to apply turning or straight ahead power simultaneously so that the whole boat responds nimbly. Depending on how fast the boat turns into the gate, how fast the current is and what direction of exit is needed, any number of stroke combinations might be required. A typical case might require two prys and/or sweeps out of each paddler before the boat is completely backward, after which they should go to a far-back simultaneously. They want to maintain downstream speed toward and through the gate, and should both try hard never to lose sight of the poles. A problem arises in that most C-boat paddlers have a hard time looking over their off-side shoulder; notice in this example the stern man is looking over his off-side shoulder during the turn into the gate but must switch shoulders to do a far-back, losing sight of the gate for an instant.

Finally, let's say a continuation of the turn is needed for the exit from this gate, so that the team is doing a full 360. The stern man should try to reach his paddle through the gate early, so he does not get jammed on the pole on his side. Having done one or two far-backs together, the paddlers have the boat about half-way through the gate now. It is time to sneak the bow out, with both paddlers leaning forward while the stern does a reverse sweep and the bow a forward sweep. This is such a powerful combination of strokes that it is quite possible to drive the bow too deep into the water, making the turn a bit sluggish. The sneak needs only to be adequate, not colossal.

On-side Reverse Spins

When you are given a choice by the circumstances whether to make an on-side or an off-side turn into a reverse gate, several factors come into the decision, including speed, helping current differentials, where the following gate is, etc. Not the least of your considerations should be how well you and your partner can see the gate in the approach. This means, all other things being equal (or even a little unequal), you should probably opt for an on-side, or "draw" turn. This means a bow-right team would do a right turn into a reverse gate, because the stern man never has to take his eye off the gate as he pulls his end in. It is more crucial for the stern man to have unimpeded sight in this case, because his end goes through the gate first! We have often heard stern men complain, after hitting a gate they were turning into with a reverse sweep, they never saw it until it was too late: in the approach they were looking over their off-side shoulder, but as the stern swung in they had to switch looking to the other shoulder, and the momentary loss of sight contact was fatal.

Doing a good on-side turn from dead upstream of a reverse gate requires the same kind of timing, teamwork and practice as described above in the section on off-side approaches. (Remember, the terms "off-side" and "on-side" in a C-2 refer to the bow man.) It is important to keep the boat flat during the turn, because burying the edge will slow the turn and can create stability problems. In the approach, the boat should be pointed off to the turning side, then turned with a strong pair of draw strokes out of each paddler. While the stern man literally pulls the stern into the gate (possibly under the inside pole), the bow man may, if the turn is going quickly, have the option of going directly to reverse strokes rather than draws to better push the boat in the desired direction, i.e., through the gate and down the river. It is crucial the bow man make a big effort to catch sight of the gate as soon as possible if he switches to looking over his on-side shoulder in this turn—it should be well before he gets to the line between the poles. The turning strokes should be done in unison, since the boat responds more consistently, and with fewer surprises, to rhythmic moves.

Hopefully, at this stage in the turn, after a couple of synchronized turning strokes, the stern man is to or even past the line between the poles. He must try hard to slide his paddle through the gate early, before his body and the wide part of the boat arrive or he will have to make an awkward, usually unsuccessful effort to avoid hitting the pole in front of him as he drifts through. Having the paddle on the far side of the gate allows him to be aggressive in completing the move and avoiding poles.

Assuming the turn must be completed as a 360, the team must now do a draw turn out. Here the biggest problems are the bow sneak and the bow man's paddle. The key to both is for the bow man to get his paddle through the gate early, before his body reaches the LBP, so that as the boat slides out of the

To the right are three photos showing an on-side reverse spin.
Photos by Doug Morriss.

gate under the pole on his side, the paddle is not only out of the way, but can help the turn and the sneak by drawing or reverse sweeping in combination with a forward lean of the paddlers' bodies. If timed properly with the stern man's forward sweep or draw, the bow will dip sufficiently to go under the pole.

The Ultimate Megastuff Slam Dunk Off-side 360

A description of the above (abbreviated UMSDOT) will finish our discussion of reverse gates. An UMSDOT will not only wow the crowd and demoralize the opposition, but might also improve your score, if the judges see the inevitable water touches as such and not as hits. Plus, it is fun to do. It is simply the ultimate gamble in an off-side reverse turn, but if practiced enough becomes less of a gamble and more the only way to do such a gate. In an UMSDOT, you sneak the inside pole right behind the stern cockpit coming in and over the bow man's thighs going out, hopefully in a total of one or two strokes, and therefore never give the ends of the boat a chance to hit the poles. You must both lean back going in, but only enough to get the stern under the pole; the tendency is to overdo it and nearly do an end-stand. Remember, the deeper the stern goes under the pole, the longer it takes to rise, and thus the longer you must wait to be able to drop the bow under the pole in the exit. You can help both actions by leaning the boat up to the bow man's side after the stern has slipped under the pole, so that the stern rises faster and the bow drops under the pole more easily as you sweep out. In this move, the last thing to leave the gate is the blade of the bow man's paddle as it digs in to complete the sweep. The wider the gate and the higher the poles, the more you should be encouraged to try an UMSDOT. Go ahead, SLAM IT HOME!

Offsets

Offset gates are difficult to do in C-2 because 1) two bodies and two paddles must make it through each gate, and 2) the weight of the whole boat gives momentum downstream, which may overtax the paddlers' ability to drive the boat sideways to the next gate. In general, C-2's should do offsets the way the other boats do, trying to complete as much of the turn toward the next gate as possible in or above the gate in question, sneaking one or both ends with the appropriate strokes,

and, in addition, working together so as not to surprise one's partner with violent, unexpected leans or strokes.

The best advice we can give here is for you and your partner to study the section on C-1 offset gates, and to discuss the strokes as you go along. You will find the strokes are very similar in C-1 and C-2, if you read in the proper sides. You must time your strokes and your sneaks effectively, so that when done together, you are clean on every pole and your lines are fast between the gates. A note of caution: sneaking both ends of a C-2 in tight offsets is very difficult but often crucial to the whole sequence; therefore, in your practice time, do not forget to allot a large portion to the practice of hard offsets.

This boat has moved too far to the right in this gate, putting the stern man in a tough position on the green pole. Photo by Eve Eaton.

Rolling a C-2

As we have said before, paddling big water and playing in a C-2 can be terrific thrills, but such fun is not available to the team that does not have a reliable roll. The best C-2 teams in the country rarely, if ever, swim, and then it is usually due to equipment problems: broken paddle, blown skirt or broken bracing. Mike and Steve Garvis nearly won a bronze medal in a team run at the 1979 World Championships after rolling up with only one paddle! (One had been dropped in the midst of an airborne switch caused by a violent wipeout.) They rolled up in big waves with Mike doing a powerful regular roll and Steve doing a hands roll timed perfectly.

Obviously, C-2's must agree in advance on which side they will roll, since communication is a bit difficult underwater! Most good teams today have foregone the cross roll in favor of a switch by the off-side paddler to his partner's side, because it is more reliable and stronger. Basically, each paddler is doing a C-1 roll on the same side, and, as we stated earlier, for some reason, it is easier to roll a close-cockpit boat than an end-hole boat. Two good C-1 rollers should have little trouble rolling a C-2.

So, the big problems in rolling a C-2 boil down to two: one person has to switch, and then the paddlers have to roll up together. The biggest timing problem comes because it takes much longer to set up to roll for the paddler on whose low brace the boat goes over. His partner can set up (switching hand positions if he is the switcher) easily as his paddle arcs through the air in the capsize. But the paddler whose paddle is buried will take some time to get organized.

Now the timing problem is crucial: who starts? Our suggestion would be for the person who has the *longest* roll to start. No banging on the boat or poking or counting; the person who is capable of sustaining the rolling power of his roll the longest should initiate the move, hoping eagerly his partner can feel the move start and join in somewhere along the way so that for enough of the time they are pushing up together. The starter (designated in advance) must think as he sets up for the roll "Is my partner ready? Was his paddle in a deep low brace as we turned over, from which it will take him a long time to get into rolling position?" If the partner is not ready, the first roll attempt is guaranteed to fail and both paddlers will spend some extra time under water without air. So, the message is clear: it is better to wait a little too long than not long enough, because the latter will definitely cause the boat to be upside down longer.

Assumed in all of this discussion on rolling is that each partner has a strong C-1 roll independently. The question often comes up as to which is better, the high-brace roll or the low-brace roll, which ends up with the non-power face of the paddle pushing down in a low brace. Our preference is to try to right the boat with the sweep and high brace, which the good teams can do consistently. If the boat is not upright at the end of the sweep, then the paddlers can turn the paddle over into a low brace and provide a powerful last-ditch effort to push the boat up before the paddle sinks to the bottom. We believe that not trying to roll the boat up on the high brace lowers the likelihood of success, since the rolling motion of the starter cannot last as long, and thus his partner has less time in which to match up the power phase of each roll. In the high-brace roll, if the starter completes his sweep and high brace before his partner catches up, there is still a chance the roll will work because the end of the starter's roll (the last ditch low brace) may match up with his partner's snap on the high brace.

Sneaking

In order to add a little perspective to the current rage for low volume boats and the "slam-dunk, double-sneak" gate technique, we hark back to 1972 and the then-awesome Augsburg slalom course. With the Olympics fast approaching and the Augsburg canal ready to eat any little boat that dared test its waters (or so we thought), U.S. boaters were frantically devising ways to *add* volume to their boats—already huge by today's standards. Two examples: Angus Morrison, super C-1 paddler, took a 73 cm Hahn C-1 and added an inch to the height of the hull. Likewise, Southworth and Burton modified a Queen Mary-size Feuillette end-hole C-2 by adding an inch to the seam. Remember, those were still the days when C-boats had the shape requirement that the ends had to be higher than any point in between (supposedly so they would retain the shape of the traditional Canadian canoe). The rules change dropping this imposition did not come until the next year, and the boats have come a long way since then. Our "fear" that the Augsburg course would demolish small boats has since been laid waste by the obvious ease with which even the smallest race boats handle the course now. Perhaps one of the reasons the East Germans did so well in the Olympics is because they had the smallest boats, correctly anticipating the advantages inherent in the smaller size and different handling characteristics.

Those were the days when canoes went *all* the way through every gate, and kayaks most of the way. Modern designs and demands for speed now require that we take advantage of every opportunity to go under a pole. Complaints that sneaking is an illegitimate whitewater technique that cheapens the quality of a slalom are anachronistic; we believe it is a good and logical result of boat and technique improvement, and that the best racers of today are more graceful, rhythmical, and beautiful to watch than ever before. Very few veteran racers have had trouble making the transition to "sneak technique"—in his little boat today Angus is still one of the best C-1 slalom paddlers in the world. The good guys still win, and would win under any rules.

A word of caution. Sneaking should be considered the "dessert" to the "meat and potatoes" of good technique. Too much sneaking and you get sick, while no sneaking leaves the meal incomplete. Everyone loves to sneak; not only does it look classy, it *feels* good. Although sneaking is now required in order to be competitive in slalom, many younger paddlers tend to overdo it in an effort to look flashy and go fast. We have seen so many people (ourselves sometimes included) pull off dramatic, usually unnecessary sneak moves during practice or low-key races. Yet, they are not quite so brave and daring during a big race! Prior to the World Championship slalom at Skopje in 1975, people looked at the easy course set

---

Tom Southworth and John Burton paddled their big-volume C-2 in the 1972 Olympics. (Next page)

407

on low water and predicted a lot of sneaking. Yet, during the race, most folks went back to the basics and took fewer risks than anticipated. The man who won in K-1, Siegbert Horn, probably did the least sneaking of anyone! He snuck a few, but he won the race with good strokes, strength, quickness, and proper positioning.

Learn the fundamentals first, and gradually incorporate an intelligent amount of sneaking into your repertoire. Remember, there is a risk in aggressive sneaking that a water touch will look too much like a boat touch for the gate judge to differentiate; you may not get the benefit of the doubt every time. Sneaking should always be a means to the end of faster times and lower scores, never an end in itself. And, never try to sneak a pole that's in the water!

Sometimes you can sneak everything under the poles. Photo by Jeff Leppo.

Team Racing

Three boats weaving their way down a slalom course in perfect position is one of the most beautiful sights in all of whitewater competition. Yet, team racing is one aspect of slalom racing which is sorely neglected by the American slalom community. A country such as England, with its strong inter-club rivalries and short distances between races, has a strong tradition in team racing and invariably does well in international team events. The English K-1 slalom team won the gold medal at the 1979 World Championships when all signs pointed toward the Austrians, who had placed three boaters in the top four in the individual event. In America, team events are usually treated lightly, and rarely do people ever practice team runs except at races.

The first thing to determine is the order in which the three boaters will run. The cleanest boater should go first, for any penalty incurred by the first boater is apt to be matched by the second or third boaters due to a swinging pole. The most experienced boater should go second, as not only does he have the course to worry about, he must also be cognizant of the actions of the first and third boaters. The fastest paddler goes last, as he must accelerate quickly upon occasion throughout the run in order to keep up with the others: All the more so if he has to drop low into an eddy due to a foul-up on the part of the first or second boater.

The standard method of going down the course involves having the second boater follow right on the heels of the first boater. The third boater leaves space between himself and the second boater, enough to allow the first boater to get in and out of an upstream gate before the third boater enters the eddy. This "standard weave" can be nerve wracking at times; another fraction of a second and the first boater would be impaled by the third boat!

Some tips on team racing:

1. Team races are most often decided on penalties rather than speed.

2. Team race pace should be about 90% of individual run pace.

3. Boater #2 will have to alter his method of negotiating upstream gates. He won't be able to dive into every upstream gate because Boater #1 may be in the gate. Also, Boater #2 will have to exit from upstream gates a few feet higher than normal in order to allow Boater #3 room to make a decent turn into the gate.

The third boat in the team race should enter an upstream gate right on the heels of the second boater. Photo by Will Summers.

The 1979 World C-1 Champions during their winning run at Jonquiere. Photo by Rita Tessmann. (Next page)

21
262
264

4. Decide as much as possible on strategy before going down the course. Don't "play it by ear," because one boater's interpretation of a situation may be entirely different from another's.

5. Teams must practice as much as possible as teams to be any good. The three best boats don't necessarily make the best team. Once three boats have found the best order in which to run, they should practice in this order as much as possible.

Practice Makes Perfect

If the opportunity for whitewater practice presents itself, don't pass it up. Good whitewater workouts with gates are few and far between, for usually the water is only up for a short period of time each year, or travel to the site may be restrictive, or the time and manpower required for setting a course may be too much for many individuals. There are so many skills to acquire on whitewater which can't be duplicated elsewhere. Some of these skills are seemingly insignificant, but they are stored away in your repertoire of technique, available for later use.

The more situations (eddies, currents, rocks) you can utilize in your practice site, the better. Of course, the best location for practice is a site which allows you to paddle from the finish up to the start. However, be sure to practice every so often on a long, drawn-out course. This will require you to get out of your boat after every run, but the simulation of the actual race is important.

If whitewater practice is unavailable, the next best thing is flatwater gate training. Don't despair if you can't practice on whitewater too often, for the old standby for developing technique is practice on flatwater gates. All the boaters of the world do far more flatwater practice than whitewater work during the year.

Whether paddling on whitewater or flatwater, prepare a specific plan for each on-the-water workout. Thirty minutes of concentrated work is far better than hours of milling about aimlessly on the gates day after day. Be sure to change the location of your practice site and/or the positioning of the gates where possible. Many boaters keep the same gates in the same position throughout the year, and as a result are able to do the gates in their sleep. In addition, keep in mind paddlers can look very good on their home practice courses. Outsiders arriving for a workout are amazed at how good the Nantahala bunch looks on the Nantahala River or the D.C. kids on their gates or the Ledyard paddlers on the gates in front of the clubhouse. Of course they look good—they've done the gates thousands of times.

While setting up your practice area, make sure your gates are as vandal-proof as possible. Tie the wires out of reach and avoid strings for pole adjustment which reach to shore and can be cut. One solution is to drive two nails into the top of each pole around which you can wrap the string for height adjustment from your boat on the river. If the strings must reach to shore, attach a shower curtain ring onto the string part-way out to the crossbar. In case someone cuts the string, the string will only slip through the eye of the crossbar up to the ring, thereby saving your pole from disappearing downstream.

Make friends with all the local kids and passersby at your practice site. Go out of your way to befriend them. Explain to them what you are doing and how much work went into setting up the course. They can make life miserable for you if they are not on your side.

The English Gate

One tried and true method for improving gate technique is the English Gate or "wiggle test." It is a standard series of maneuvers in and around a single gate hung over flatwater, and thus has the great advantage of being useful in a very confined body of water. The movements are standard throughout the world, and involve all the strokes you are likely to have to use in a slalom race.

You will find the discussion that follows to be extremely detailed and complete. The intention is not to imply that the English Gate should dominate your practice hours, but is to say that working on the English Gate can add real precision to your technique and can serve as a valuable reference to other practice and race situations. Beginning racers would do well to master moves required in the English Gate.

The four "phases" of the English Gate require mastery of the four basic direction-change skills in slalom racing: changing forward speed in one direction to forward speed the other way (Phase I), changing forward speed to backward speed (Phase II), changing backward speed in one direction to backward speed the other way (Phase III), and changing backward speed to forward speed (Phase IV). Stated another way, Phases I & III involve turning, Phases II & IV are "stop-start."

Phase I. Starting with the nose of your boat on the gate line, go forward through, turn left, forward through, turn right, forward through (3 passes altogether—the other three phases have two passes each, making a total of 9 times through the gate).

Phase II. Stop the boat as abruptly as possible after the stern has cleared (either through or out to one side under a pole), and back the boat down the outside of one side of the gate at top speed. Roll to the inside, stopping the boat's backward momentum with the sweep stroke of your roll so that the bow clears the pole by an inch; now drive the boat forward through the gate, at an angle toward the other side, so that you can, after another abrupt stop, back the boat down the outside of the other pole, roll to the inside again, then drive the boat through the gate. This is your fifth pass through the gate, and you are facing the same direction as when you started.

A pull-draw combination stroke, used to sink the bow and start the boat moving forward down the outside of the gate, is commonly used in the English Gate.

Phase III. Stop the boat abruptly again, and back down the outside of the gate for the third time, but this time spin the boat by pulling the stern into the gate and back through. Now quickly spin the bow out of the gate the opposite way of the previous spin, and quickly back through the gate for your seventh pass.

Phase IV. You've just cleared the LBP (Line between the poles) with your bow—now stop the boat and draw the bow to one side with one stroke, pass outside the gate, roll to the inside, then back through the gate. Use your head underwater—don't roll up with a huge forward sweep, because you will just propel yourself away from the gate. Do a slap roll and come up looking back over your inside shoulder and paddling backwards. Don't wait until you bounce off the pool gutter while shaking water out of your hair before you start looking around for the gate. Complete the English Gate by going forward around the outside of the other pole, rolling to the inside, then backing through the gate. Nine passes in all, 5 forward, 4 reverse, 4 rolls, no penalties, 70 seconds! Right!?

How to Use the English Gate for Technique

Many people consider the English Gate a boring, repetitive, grunt exercise of limited value. We, who between us have done many hundreds of English Gates, consider it an extremely valuable, challenging, and intellectual exercise, of which very few people take maximum advantage. It is indeed repetitive—and it is astounding to see how many people do nothing but repeat mistakes, without thinking. Suggestions:

1) Plan your lines. Move from one side of the gate to the other on planned diagonals, cutting down the distance travelled. For example, start Phase III by going backwards down the opposite side of the gate from your last move in Phase II—this means you must start Phase II on that side. If you are a righty C-1, you will want to start Phase II by going around the left pole (as you face the gate at the start), so that you can also start Phase III on that side. Reason: The first spin in Phase III is much more controllable with your blade to the inside of the turn, looking over your inside (right) shoulder. Think about it.

2) Plan your positions. Remember when you roll to the inside, the

boat actually travels that way a bit, rather than corkscrewing along a straight line. This means that in Phase IV, as you roll over after passing by the pole, your boat will tend to move into the pole—be careful. This is related to planning your lines: you want to complete a move through or around the gate in the best position to start the next move. Example: in completing Phase III, you should be backing toward one side or the other as you pass through the gate, so that you have the easiest possible move to the outside of the gate to begin Phase IV.

3) Plan your strokes. You should strive for perfection in your English Gate work to the extent that a video tape of one English Gate should be indistinguishable from a live telecast of the next. This means that *every stroke* is planned, and, for an expert English Gater, done the same way in the same sequence every time. When you get tired this won't happen, but it should be your goal—you should take deep, powerful, significant strokes, and they should be the same ones in every English Gate you do! Example: Plan a right turn for your first move; in a kayak, this should mean your first four strokes are forward on the right, forward on the left, forward on the right, reverse sweep on the right. If you really accelerate the boat quickly, you might not need the first stroke on the right: start with a left stroke. Example: in Phase IV, in the transition from backward through the gate to forward around the outside of the pole, your best stroke to either side is a forward draw on the outside; i.e., if you are going to the right of the gate for your first outside pass, go from back to forward with a right forward stroke that draws the bow just to the right of the pole, then rips the boat up the outside of the gate. The incorrect stroke is a forward stroke or sweep on the left, which turns the boat too much without pulling the center of the boat (the paddler) to the outside of the pole.

The difference may not look like much but really is. This move is to be followed by a roll, then a backward pass through the gate, and the positional superiority is obvious. The boat is farther along in its pass outside the gate, because the right side stroke can be done longer and stronger and really pull the boat forcefully.

4) Keep your eye on the gate. Practice correct head movement, so you do not look like you are responding negatively to a question when you are really trying to see both poles. Remember, if you can see one pole, you should know where the other one is. Done properly, the English Gate teaches you to be able to look over the correct shoulder in approaching reverse gates, and gives practice on both sides. Example: in Phase IV, as you pass outside the right pole, keep your eye on that pole, then as you back through the gate keep looking over your left shoulder. On your next pass, around the left side and then through the gate, keep looking over your right shoulder.

5) NEVER QUIT an English Gate you have started, whether timed or not. So often the guy who tries to "win the practices" will

plead "let me start over again" after he slams the pole with his stern on the first pass! The goal in the end is always the big white-water race, not the hot English Gate, so remember, the English Gate is a means, not an end. This does not mean you should not really hustle and try like fury to do it clean, but it does mean you cannot abandon an English Gate that will not be your best because of a penalty. You must prepare yourself for actual racing, where no one who has hit gate 1 has gotten a sympathetic ear from the starter by saying "Aw, cmon, lemme start again!" The excuse of "My whole run was fouled up because I hit gate one" gets no sympathy either—the guy's opponents shake their heads silently, realizing they have a psychological advantage over him, because he can be rattled.

You can and must develop a mental toughness about such early mistakes by being tough on yourself in practice, including in timed English Gates. This means that you must finish, with the lowest *total* score possible, any English Gate you start. If you swing a pole, do your damnedest to avoid it on your next pass—or, if you're really in control but cannot avoid hitting it (being hit by it, in this case), try to make the second hit dampen the movement of the pole. Don't react in anger, but in a cool, businesslike way—your ability to avoid a swinging pole in a pool may make the difference in a race when you catch a slow boater in front of you or encounter lots of wind.

When you find yourself on a windy course, where your competitors are psyched out and griping like crazy, you should be saying to yourself: "Super—I've got the swinging pole routine down pat, I've done it so much in the pool (not too much we hope). This makes it interesting, and the challenge of timing passes through the gates is the same for everyone." If you have the psychological advantage, or just think you have, you have a leg up on your competitors. You will often hear that the guy with only a few penalties on a windy course was just lucky—don't believe it for a minute.

How to Use the English Gate for Conditioning

We cannot emphasize enough the importance of doing planned slalom workouts instead of sessions filled with random wanderings. Your plan early in the season, or after an injury, or after an all-nighter with the books, or after a big race, might be a workout of long, slow sequences done in a physically "quiet" way. These can be great and very useful for technique and attitude rejuvenation, but don't avoid imposing at least a minimum of order on the workout—plan 10 slow repetitions of each of two 10-gate sequences, then call it a day.

Most of the time, your slalom gate work should be physically demanding, and if a single flatwater or pool gate is all you have, the English Gate can provide all the rigor you are willing to let it. How about a pyramid, that we have used many times? Single, double, triple, quadruple, triple, double, single, all timed and scored, with 1-2 minutes rest between each set. That's a total of 16 timed English Gates (you may not want to do 64 Eskimo Rolls, so leave out the roll on some). A double English Gate means two in a row, non-stop, maximum effort. (Don't hit the poles!) The great thing about an all-out English Gate workout is that it is pure—no distractions, no rests for your muscles, since the paddle is *always* working, and you are always pulling or pushing.

What's a good time to shoot for? It's hard to know in these days of high poles and super sneak boats, but 10 years ago, in the pre-sneak days, Eric did a 58 in his kayak and John a 66 in his C-1, both with rolls. Without rolls it should be 3-6 seconds faster (John did all the rolls in his C-1 to his on-side). You should try to generalize from this very detailed description of English Gates, applying the advice here about lines, timing, angles, and planning to gate sequence workouts and to races as well. Precision is a must in all of them, and the little hints offered in this section can well be used in thinking about all sorts of slalom gate combinations.

English Gates are an old standby when time, space and manpower are limited. You can always drop a gate from a bridge or tree and get in a workout. One summer on Lake Winnipesaukee, Eric worked at a summer camp, and overhanging trees, bridges, etc., were not available. He cut down two small trees, delimbed them and implanted them near shore. With those two sticks protruding from the water, he practiced daily on the English Gate for eight straight weeks. If he hit the sticks too many times in a row they would fall over in the water—that was the deterrent to pole touching. Of course, when you're 15 and hungrier than hell, nothing can stop you.

The English Gate teaches you a sense of where you are in the gate. After doing a lot of them you will develop a feel for where your boat is and how much of it is left in the gate before you can start turning. It is also a great way to practice quick body thrusts which can actually move your boat forward or backward a few inches and away from a pole if all else fails. Try it yourself. Place your bow very close to one side of a pole and one or two inches beyond it. With a violent backward thrust of your body, without using your paddle, move the bow around the pole to the other side. Do the same with the stern.

Another trick for avoiding a touch is to dip or raise one side of your boat when a pole threatens to hit the side, especially near your body. Raising or lowering one side will make the boat narrower and just might provide the extra inch you need for clearance.

"It's Great To Be the Best—CCA"

The most appropriate way to wrap up this chapter on slalom technique is to look at the best paddlers in the world and analyze how they got there. We refer to the "kids" from the Canoe Cruisers Association in Washington, D.C., and their incredible success in recent years.

First, a tribute to the individuals and their accomplishments in 1979:

Cathy Hearn—triple World Champion in 1979! Photo by Jon Nelson.

Cathy Hearn—the third person in history to win three gold medals in a single World Championships, Cathy in 1979 won the slalom individual, the slalom team with Linda Harrison and Becky Judd, and the wildwater team with Carol Fisher and Leslie Klein. Cathy is 21, and was 10th in the 1977 World Championships, her first.

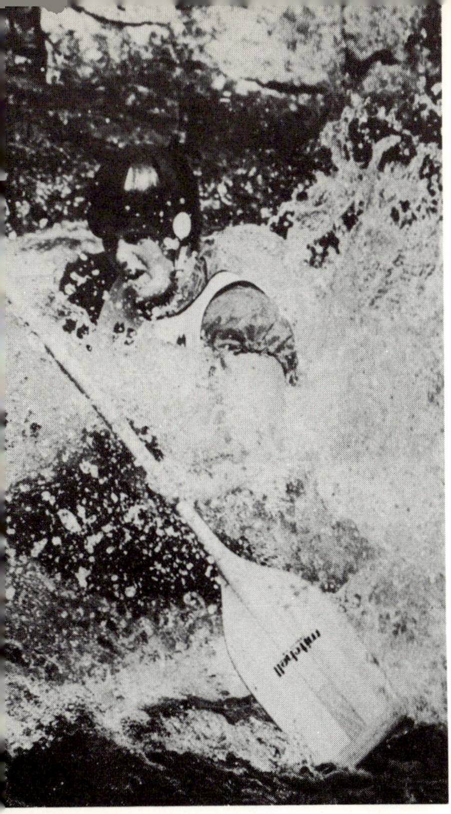

Jon Lugbill—Jon dominated the C-1 class at Jonquiere, winning the individual slalom title on both runs and leading the slalom team to the gold, where they won by 60 points on their *poorer* run, 70 points on their best run. Jon showed the world an aggressive style that makes him incredibly fast, and, at Jonquiere, he finally realized his awesome potential. Jon is 19, in his third World Championships!

1979 C-1 World Slalom Champion Jon Lugbill. Photo by Jeff Leppo.

David Hearn—Cathy's brother did pretty well himself, with a silver medal, four seconds behind Jon in C-1 slalom, and the team gold with Jon and Bobby Robison. David has been the most consistent paddler over the last two seasons; Jon had to be at the top of his form to beat him. In 1979, David was in his second World Championships.

David Hearn—a gold and a silver at Jonquiere. Photo by Eve Eaton.

56

Bob Robison—Bumbo is the blueprint for the big-race performer who does his best when the pressure is greatest. The first time Bob *placed* in an American race in 1979 was at the team trials, where a brilliant run at the end of the second and crucial day left him third boat on the team. He followed that up with the bronze medal in the C-1 slalom individuals and two superb runs in the team race with Jon and David. Bob is 18, and Jonquiere was his second World Championships; in his first, in 1977, he was a surprise fourth, after being as big a surprise fourth in the U.S. team trials. His bronze medal in '79, however, was not a surprise.

These four are the double medal winners produced by the CCA in 1979. The only single medal winner was Kent Ford, who helped the C-1 wildwater team to a silver medal, missing the gold by half a second. Kent also missed making the slalom team by three tenths of a second on a total of 441 seconds.

Bob Robison—fourth in the Worlds in 1977, third in 1979, gold medal in the 1979 C-1 Slalom Team race. Photo by Eve Eaton.

5
18

Kent Ford—a genius in both slalom and wildwater. Photo by Jeff Leppo.

Other CCA performers: Ron Lugbill placed fifth in C-1 slalom, and Kent Ford placed eighth in C-1 wildwater. The men kayakers did not win any medals, but the best performances on the U.S. team at Jonquiere, and the best individual performances ever in the respective classes, were turned in by CCA paddlers Chris McCormick (5th in K-1 slalom) and Dan Schnurrenburger (8th in K-1 wildwater). These guys came remarkably close to winning medals.

The top American slalom C-2 was the CCA team of Mike and Steve Garvis in 12th place, which was well below their ability, demonstrated by their fourth in the 1977 Worlds and their very decisive win at the 1978 pre-Worlds at Jonquiere. Quite simply, the Garvi had a bad weekend, at the wrong time. Carl Gutschick and Paul Flack were 16th in C-2 in the World Championships, also a disappointment, since they had paddled much better at the team trials six weeks earlier. Dan Isbister and Tom McGowan of the CCA were 22nd and 47th in K-1 slalom, major disappointments and also below their demonstrated ability levels. The other CCA boats in the World Championships were wildwater C-2's, Jef Huey and Paul Grabow, and David Hearn and Ron Lugbill, 12th and 13th respectively.

Ten of the 16 boats on the slalom team were from the CCA, including all of the individual medal winners except Linda Harrison, who was third in K-1W for the second time in a row. What has caused this incredible surge of power? It is a combination of circumstances, some obvious, some mysterious.

1) Ability. Every one of the paddlers mentioned is very talented, and thus able to perform the most complicated and difficult moves.

2) Experience. The "kids" have done an astounding amount of racing, even as young as they are. They have also been paddling from an early age. The Lugbill brothers appeared in their first World Championships in C-2 slalom at the ages of 14 and 16!

3) Dedication. These folks paddle their hearts out in workouts, then paddle some more. They are very singleminded, and for the last several years have concentrated on little else but whitewater training and racing.

4) Facilities. In the Washington, D.C. area they have at their disposal great indoor and outdoor paddling facilities in the David Taylor Model Basin (a huge naval testing "pool"), and the Potomac River, which is great for slalom training in some places and for bigwater playing in others.

5) Support. This comes in large doses from their families and from their club, who provide enough moral, logistical, and financial support to make training a full-time pursuit.

6) Competition. Within the club, as we have seen, are many of the best racers in the world, especially in C-1. They train together, experimenting always with technique to find that little edge that pushes them ahead, never letting up because there are always a few hot paddlers right behind. The list of CCA paddlers who just missed making the 1979 team is fairly awesome in itself: the fifth boat in *every* class at the team trials was a CCA paddler!

7) Last, but far from least, coaching. Bill Endicott, U.S. team member in C-2 in 1971 and 1973, alternate to the 1972 Olympic Team, has added an immeasurable dimension of quality, organization and dedication to the overall effort of these young paddlers. Bill spends untold hours by the poolside and river bank organizing workouts, working on techniques, pushing the paddlers to get the most out of themselves and providing structure to a bunch of stalwart individualists. His contribution cannot be overemphasized, because he has been at it for several years now and has influenced these kids over a significant portion of their competitive careers. The example of hard work and dedication he sets is an inspiration to all of them, and now it has been shown his methods work. Bill deserves much credit, and he should be justifiably proud of all he and his charges have ac-

complished. We now know how important a disciplined, concerned, talented coach can be in our sport. With the growth in numbers and strength of the CCA program under Bill Endicott, we have our first really competitive training and racing environment in the U.S. We now know this is what it takes to be the best in the world.

Training Camps

One of the problems facing paddlers in this country is the distance separating the various paddling centers. Racers in the Pacific Northwest rarely paddle with Easterners except under race conditions. Nantahala paddlers face a 10-hour drive to get to Washington, D.C. and vice versa. Conducting training camps which bring together paddlers from different areas into a single, controlled environment of sharing and learning is one of the best ways to raise the overall level of ability of the paddlers present at the camp. These paddlers, in turn, can return home and disseminate their newly acquired knowledge to the locals.

There are several observations which should be made with regard to training camps.

1. Each training camp should have specific goals relative to the people in attendance and the time of year when it is held. A winter training camp should emphasize conditioning and technique while a summer camp should emphasize speed and timed runs.

2. Since most people train on flatwater at home, it makes sense to have a training camp on good whitewater if at all possible.

3. Training camps should be no longer than 5-7 days. Boredom and physical fatigue will set in after a week. In addition, be wary of scheduling a training camp after a major race or Trials. The weekend wear and tear of a major race where emotions run high demands a rest period and settling back to earth of the paddlers before another stressful situation, such as a training camp, takes place.

4. Beware of overtraining during the first two days of the camp. Don't work to exhaustion on Monday and Tuesday of a week-long camp because you'll really be dragging by Thursday and Friday. A good case in point was the highly successful Eastern Team training camp held in April, 1979 after the Tariffville race. Enthusiasm was high, the water was good and there were 30 gates ready to be used. Monday morning saw us all up early for a pre-breakfast run. The morning workout was timed runs over the full length of the course. In the afternoon, it was more timed runs over a short, 8-10 gate sequence. Since it was a nice day, most of the boaters stayed out on the water playing in the waves and doing pop-ups. Tuesday's schedule was much the same. By Wednesday, most people were too pooped to derive much benefit from the second workout of the day. And many people took Thursday off entirely due to fatigue.

It would have been better to back off a little on Monday and Tuesday, thereby saving some strength to ensure some good sessions later in the week.

Whitewater Slalom Racing Rules

Article 21. Negotiation of Gates

1. All gates must be negotiated in numerical order. Forward gates shall be negotiated in accordance with the colors, bow first. Reverse gates shall be negotiated in accordance with the colors, stern first.

2. Negotiation of a gate begins when the gate is *engaged,* which means either of the following:

a) A pole is touched by boat, paddler, or paddle;

b) The head or torso of the competitor (in C-2 either competitor) has broken the line between the poles (gate line).

3. Negotiation of a gate is *completed* when either of the following applies:

a) The head and entire torso of the paddler (in C-2 both paddlers) and part of the boat has crossed the gate line in the correct direction *and* the boat has continued through, either onwards or sidewards, and left the gate line (a hand, arm, or paddle remaining within the gate after the boat and torso have cleared is not considered when judging completion);

b) A 50-second penalty is incurred by any of the means described in Article 22.A.4 through 22.A.9.

4. Negotiation of a gate is *correct* when it occurs as described in Article 21.3a, provided that no 50-second penalty is incurred by any of the means described in Article 22.A.4 through 22.A.9. Negotiation of a gate is *faultless* when, in addition to being *correct,* neither pole has been touched by the boat, paddler, or paddle.

5. Negotiation of the Team Gate must be completed by all three boats of a team within 15 seconds. The time will start from the moment the first team member engages the Team Gate, and will end when the third team member has completed negotiation of the gate. In addition, if any team member incurs a 50-second penalty by any of the means described in Article 22.A, sections 4, 5, 7, or 8, then the 50-second team penalty (Article 22.A.10) will also be assessed.

Article 22. Judging

A. Penalties

Penalties are not cumulative at a single gate. If more than one infraction occurs, only the one highest penalty is assessed.

1. No penalty—Faultless negotiation.

2. 10 second penalty—Correct negotiation, but touching one pole.

3. 20 second penalty—Correct negotiation, but touching both poles.

4. 50 second penalty—Gate engaged but not negotiated. Lack of negotiation is judged to have occurred only when the competitor engages the next following gate in the numerical order, or clearly abandons the attempt and continues down the course.

5. 50 second penalty—Intentional pushing aside of a pole in an attempt to lessen a penalty. This penalty is assessed only if the intentional pushing materially affects the negotiation of the gate.

6. 50 second penalty—Eskimo rolling while the body (in C-2 either body or between the bodies) is within the gate. A roll is judged to have occurred if the entire torso (trunk of the body, not including arms and head) of the competitor (in C-2 either competitor) is momentarily under water.

7. 50 second penalty—Negotiation of a gate contrary to the color indications or the R sign according to Article 21.1. A contrary negotiation is judged to have occurred if at any instant, during the passage of the head and torso of the competitor (in C-2 both competitors) between the poles, the boat is situated contrary to the colors or the R sign.

8. 50 second penalty—Gate omitted. A gate is judged to have been omitted only when the competitor engages the next following gate in the numerical order, or clearly abandons the attempt and continues down the course.

9. 50 second penalty—Repeated attempt at a gate after the body of the competitor (in C-2 either competitor) has broken the gate line. This means that once a competitor has broken the gate line he must continue onward until clear of the gate without dropping back or moving sidewards such that his body leaves the gate. In the case of an upstream gate in current, if dropping back is so minor as to have occurred between normal paddling strokes, it is not to be judged a repeated attempt. In C-2 neither body may drop back so as to leave the gate line, nor may the boat leave the gate sideways after one body has crossed and then return.

10. 50 second penalty—Failure to negotiate the Team Gate in accordance with Article 21.5. This penalty is assessed to the team as a whole, in addition to any individual penalties incurred on the Team Gate.

B. Interpretations:

1. Once negotiation of a gate is completed (Article 21.3), that gate is immediately dead and no further penalties can be incurred.

2. The *gate line* is an imaginary line drawn between the tips of the two poles at any instant, whether they are hanging straight down or have been brought into motion by wind or contact. An imaginary extension of a

pole may be needed to define the gate line in some cases involving large motions.

3. Passing underneath a pole without touching (undercutting) is not penalized.

4. In all doubtful or borderline cases, the competitor is given the benefit of the doubt and the lower penalty. For example:

a) If a Judge is in doubt as to whether movement of a pole was caused by contact or by a water splash, no penalty for a pole touch may be given.

b) With regard to forward or reverse negotiation, when the boat is so nearly broadside that correct or incorrect direction cannot be determined, benefit of doubt is given.

5. Repeated attempts at a gate are not penalized provided the body of the competitor (in C-2 either body) has not broken the gate line.

6. If a gate is engaged out of numerical order, the following applies:

a) One gate omitted: This is penalized according to Article 22.A.8 as omitted. Any penalty incurred on the gate engaged out of order stands.

b) Two or more gates omitted: The penalty on the gate engaged out of order can be nullified by going back and negotiating any *one or more* of the gates omitted. Each gate finally omitted is penalized according to Article 22.A.8.

7. In addition to the interpretations listed here, there shall be a series of numbered diagrams which shall depict various judging situations. These shall be considered an integral part of these rules.

C. Placement of Judges

Judging stations, or individual Gate Judges, must be located so that all situations can be clearly observed. Particular attention must be given to having a Judge exactly on the gate line where problems of boat orientation are likely to be severe, or where a post-negotiation touch may occur as at some upstream gates. It is advised that Judges have two distinct viewpoints for each gate when possible. Judges must also have some view of preceding and following sections of the course in order to judge omitted gates according to Articles 22.A.8 and 22.B.6.

3

Slalom Racing—The Final Steps

Race day is a day of opportunity. It is a chance to demonstrate the highest level of paddling of which you are capable. It is here where you can reveal the depth and quality of your training program. Most uniquely, it is an opportunity to measure yourself against the competition, to compare your ability with that of your peers. If we were not competitive, if we did not want these comparisons, we could do all our paddling alone with no one watching and no one timing, and be content in our own personal creativity and joy of movement.

However, it is safe to say that most of us have a certain measure of competitiveness and we need and/or enjoy the black and white result sheet which compares us with others to see where we stand, to have a goal for all the training. Slalomists need audience or peer approval as do actors performing in a play or painters displaying their work in a gallery exhibit. And, like any play or exhibit, a slalom will make unique logistical demands on you if you are to take full advantage of your preparation time and effort. Details, details, details. The paddler who leaves nothing to chance in the few days prior to the race is the one most likely to realize his maximum potential on race day.

Race day will not "take care of itself" just because you followed sound training habits. You must plan to make it the best racing day possible for you under the circumstances. Proper physical and mental preparation are of course essential; the final steps to a successful race are the seemingly small details which go unnoticed if they are handled well, but which can ruin a good opportunity if they are ignored.

Common sense and attention to detail in situations which arise at all races will have you preparing for nearly all your races in the same ways. Some preparations will differ according to how important the race is to you, which, it must be emphasized, is entirely personal. What you may see as being important is entirely independent of what others think. So, if a race is "unimportant" to you, it is unimportant where you finish in the results. You will be training through the race, using it as a part of your preparation for future events. If the race is "all-important," such as a World Championship or an off-year National Championship, you will be pointing for it all year, and will try to be at your peak in all ways for it. Most races fall in between, so that you care very much where you finish and how well you perform on the scoreboard, but have other races to worry about subsequently.

We will be discussing here general guidelines for the final preparation and racing strategy in the average, "important" race. We would like to emphasize that while it is of course wise to train harder for the bigger races, it is not necessarily smart to prepare "harder." We speak from the experience of the 1969 World Championships, where both of us were in superb physical shape and psyched up to do our best. We made the critical mistake of building the race up in our minds way out of proportion, and felt compelled to prepare for it in all sorts of special ways. We tightened ourselves into our bracing arrangements to make sure we had that extra feel for the boats, we snugged up our spray skirts and life jackets. We wore super light clothing we had never tried before, we did a special warm-up, ate special meals, changed to new paddles at the last minute, you name it—we did it differently or more thoroughly than ever before. It's a wonder we even made it to gate one; we felt awkward in our boats because we weren't used to being in them so tightly. We could hardly breathe because our spray covers and life jackets were too tight, we were tired from our warm-up—a disaster all the way around. If we had gone about our business normally, as we would at the Savage or the Mascoma, we would have been a lot better off.

Therefore, you should develop sound habits in race preparation and follow them for all your races. Train soundly, prepare logically, and race intelligently and you will do your best at each race.

In the days leading up to the race, there are certain logistical problems which must be sorted out so that you are free to concentrate on racing during the weekend. Attention to detail will reap rewards. Most of these details will be an outgrowth of good common sense, yet it is surprising how many paddlers ruin months of training by a lack of follow-up on race day. Here is a series of questions you can refer to as race day approaches.

The Week Before

Equipment

Does your boat conform to race regulations? Is the flotation adequate? Grab loops secure and large enough? Check the boat for leaks, weak spots, blown seams, loose seats, and weak foot braces.

Is your paddle sound? Repair it if necessary, bring a spare to the race, and have your spare near the start in case you break yours warming up. If your life jacket is going to be tested, will it float? More important, will it float you if you swim?

Do you have enough warm, dry clothing for lousy weather? (If you are going to the Mascoma, the weather will be lousy—cold rain or snow—no doubt about it!) You should take more changes of clothes than you think you will need, because it is always great to change into something completely dry after practice runs and between race runs, and that takes lots of clothes if it's a two-day race.

Transportation, Food, Lodging

How are you going to drive to the race? Now is the time to arrange for a ride or for riders in your car. Scrambling around for a ride on Friday night will only raise your anxiety level.

Are you going to cook your meals or eat at a local spot, or a combination of the two? Some folks plan on taking food for breakfast and lunch and eating at a restaurant for the evening meal.

Where are you going to sleep? Call ahead if you are staying with a friend, or make advance reservations for a campsite or motel.

Race Details

Has your entry been accepted? When and where does the race start? Which events are on which days? Can you practice the day before on the course? When will the water be running?

If you live near the race site, you would be wise to paddle on the slalom course water as much as possible during the week prior to the race. (But be careful of losing your "sharpness," which can be maintained only by paddling in gates.) Get a feel for the water even if you have no idea where the gates will be situated. If there is a particularly bad section or big roller, work it over backwards and forwards so you feel comfortable on it and so that no gate combination will surprise you. Ease off in your training in the latter part of the week. Hard workouts are O.K. on Monday and Tuesday, but you should begin tapering Wednesday, down to complete rest on Friday (and maybe Thursday, too, depending on how you feel).

Eric Evans has his boat measured prior to the 1974 Nationals in Buena Vista, Colo.

The Day Before

Your actions this day will depend to a large extent on how long your drive is to the race and on whether there is unlimited practice on the course.

If there is just one official practice run, called a "non-stop" (in French it is pronounced "non-stop"), there is no need to arrive early at the race site the day before the race. Allow yourself enough time/daylight to set your camp and have a thorough look at the course from both sides of the river. Memorize all the gates, drawing a map if necessary, and don't go to bed without knowing the course.

If there is unlimited practice, by all means take advantage of it if you can. Work over the gates as much as possible. Try every conceivable way of doing each sequence. See what you can get away with on the gates and what you can't.

Follow your normal schedule in eating and sleeping. Slalom racing does not require a special diet, unlike marathon running where carbohydrate loading may be of benefit. Tom Southworth once mentioned that he ate more in the days prior to the race in anticipation of not having the chance to eat much on race day. As a last reminder, pick up your number and find your work assignment, and dry your clothes for tomorrow.

If you feel like having a beer the night before, go ahead. It goes without saying that tying one on the night before does not make good sense, but a beer or two might help you relax and sleep better.

Race Day

Breakfast on race day will depend on the time of your first run. If it is early in the morning, you will want to have a small breakfast and grab something to eat between runs if time allows. It is always wise to eat too little rather than too much on race day. However, if you don't race until late morning or afternoon, eat your normal breakfast and plan a light lunch.

If there is unlimited practice, and you weren't able to be on the water the day before, get out on the water early and work over the course (the earlier the better, as there will be less traffic). Usually three or four runs will do the trick—much more than that and you run the risk of becoming tired for the actual event.

A "non-stop" practice run demands special attention. It is usually held early in the morning, and means that each competitor is allowed only one run on the course, and within that run, only one pass at each gate. Since this is such a limited opportunity, you must make good use of it; make sure you have the course memorized and watch as many boaters run before you as you can, realizing that weaker, less experienced boaters make the moves look hard and the experts make them look easy. You must be able to gauge from this what you will be capable of doing. It is best to treat the practice run like a race run and attack it with the same speed. Only by going all out can you judge which strokes to use and how close to cut each gate. Also, a hard maneuver at the bottom of the course is going to feel different when you are tired than when you are fresh, and the only way to appreciate the level of fatigue you are going to have at that stage is to experience it during your practice run. Many boaters, after floating through the course on their practice run, can pull off a great move at gate 25. Yet, in their race run, they don't quite pull it off because they couldn't do it when they were tired.

During a practice run consider cutting the gates a bit too close to see what you can get away with; you may discover that a certain move is easier than it looks from shore. Remember, you will be able to make the best judgments in advance if you make the effort to look at the course from both sides of the river, even if it is inconvenient to get to the far bank.

Warming Up and Warming Down

The purpose of a warm-up is to prepare yourself both mentally and physically for the acute demands of a four-minute slalom. In general, try to raise a sweat during your warm-up, allowing two-three minutes to settle down before your run. Most of us do not warm up enough before a run, finding we don't loosen up properly until after the run is over. You have done enough training to stand a vigorous couple of minutes of exercise before your race, so do not be afraid to limber up completely.

PFD measuring at the 1973 National Championships.

The ideal warm-up should start about 20 minutes before your run. You will need more time in cold weather, and more time early in the day than late. Start off with a brisk run and some dry-land calisthenics and stretching exercises. Once on the water, stretch out slowly until you are doing a series of short, hard sprints and quick turns. Play in the waves and develop a feel for the water. Try to relax and concentrate. Take some sand or mud in your hands and rub the paddle shaft where you grip it to obtain the best possible hold before you start.

A proper warm-up will also relieve nervous tension to some extent. Go through the course in your mind, thinking about your actions on the course, not the result of your actions. Make sure your spray skirt is on correctly.

It is only natural to watch a few of the boaters ahead of you as they take off from the start and do the first few gates. Keep in mind that everybody can look fast and clean at the start. You will, too.

After the race run, allow your body to cool down slowly by paddling easily for a few minutes. In most races, you will have to wait at the finish line for a few minutes as a safety boat for those following you, and you should make use of this time as a warm-down. A good warm-down will allow the blood to keep circulating and carry away lactic acid which accumulated in your muscles during the race.

During Your Run

What is the optimum mental state for a good slalom run? "Cool, controlled aggression" describes it pretty well. You want to attack the course and take advantage of every opportunity to save time, but you cannot afford to thrash blindly at your maximum stroke rate in gates. If you go to "Plan B," which has come to mean the all-out attempt for speed, you will inevitably hit a pole or two, or miss a move and blow by several gates. Paddlers usually resort to Plan B after hitting a pole early in a run, which is just plain bad strategy. If a ten-penalty run will win the race, it should not matter whether it occurs on gate one or gate 30, but it is surprising how many top paddlers will abandon their cool, calm, "controlled aggression" race strategy after an early penalty and switch to Plan B, which usually means sacrificing the run altogether.

You must learn to forget your mistakes immediately in a slalom race, because otherwise your concentration cannot be exclusively on the immediate task at hand, which it must be. Many race courses (among them, the Savage) can have some of their toughest moves in the first three or four gates, so even if a clean run is a realistic expectation, you should not abandon all hope of winning or placing or doing well after an early penalty. Your competitors are likely to earn a penalty there also. Jamie McEwan won the 1973 C-1 slalom Nationals even though he took a 50-point penalty on gate one on both runs!

The best racers in the country are those who cannot be rattled, whose concentration on the course is unbreakable and directed completely to the handling of the next few gates in sequence. Your mental "horizon" while on the course should be just the challenge of the next sequence of gates and moves. This of course is a constantly changing horizon, for the instant you are through a gate or off a wave you must forget it, and as you are working through a gate or a turn the "horizon" moves on to include the following problem. Thought of in this way, as a constantly evolving series of small, manageable problems, a slalom course is much more "handleable" than when viewed as a complex whole. Once you have memorized a course thoroughly, you must begin to think of it in pieces, in two- or three- or four-gate combinations. It is much easier, then, to race it a piece at a time, thinking ahead only far enough to anticipate the proper lines to the subsequent gates.

Essential, then, to a successful slalom run is total concentration on the task—the ability to ignore distractions. Some of those distractions are: being totally inundated by a wave, hitting a submerged rock unexpectedly, getting a "lousy" ten because the wind blew the pole into you, hearing cheers from shore after you pull off a slick move, hearing a recognizable voice yell at you, missing a move you thought you had wired, overtaking or being overtaken by an opponent, having a clean run through the hardest section of the course, and many others. You must develop the ability to "race through" all these distractions, to stick to your plan through the last gate and across the finish line. Only then can you look up, shout, curse, pound the deck, or smile.

Between Runs

You should spend the time after your first run preparing for your second run. The first run is history and agonizing over it is useless. However, agonizing is not the same thing as analyzing, and analyzing means learning from your mistakes on the first run so that your second run is even better.

The first thing you should do is change completely into dry clothes. In cold weather this can mean a hat, sweater, parka, pants, and boots if necessary. Be sure that you are warm and not shivering in wet tennis sneakers.

Make sure your boat and equipment are brought up to the start or warm-up area. If you had trouble with a certain gate combination, watch other people on the course and see if you can pick up a pointer. Beware of chasing up and down the bank watching other racers and worrying over how they are doing. Try to pick out one or two key spots and sit down and watch. A lot of energy can be needlessly wasted by constantly pacing the riverbank between runs.

If the weather is hot, stay in the shade. Better yet, lie down in a cool, quiet place and gather your thoughts for the second run. Drink some fluids if you are thirsty, but beware of eating as there will not be enough time for digestion before your second run.

Of course, it is only natural to see how you stand in relation to others by checking the scoreboard. Plan your strategy for the second run based on what you see on the scoreboard and how you feel. However, keep in mind that most people will have better second runs.

Strategy

Your aim for this race is to win and the level of competition today demands that you make maximum use of the two chances given you. In other words, "go for it" on both runs. The days of putting a clean run in the bank are pretty much gone. By having a clean, fast run on your first try, you immediately put the pressure on your competition. Then you have nothing to lose by taking a few more chances on your second run. Keep in mind that most people improve on their second runs as a result of knowing the course that much better (with a practice run and a race run under their belts). Never underestimate anybody and be aware that the race isn't over until the last boater's time is posted and all protests are settled. Eric had the 1968 Nationals in the bag and everybody was congratulating him as the last boater went down the course. That boater, Roger Paris, won by .6 of a second.

Courtesy and Work Details

Anyone who has organized a slalom knows the incredible amount of work involved. Most competitors are assigned a work detail during the weekend, and it certainly makes for a smooth race when everyone does his job. Make sure you do your assignment and pitch in when the need arises.

Many people have the impression that they won the race because, naturally, they were better. In today's competition, a person is more likely to win because all the other people lost. In other words, your success at a particular race may have been due to someone else's misfortune and the tables will be turned next time. Don't give anybody an axe to grind by excessive screaming and yelling after you have won—it will only make people want to beat you more the next time. "Keep your words soft and sweet, you never know which ones you'll have to eat." Courtesy and good manners are their own reward, but have you ever noticed who gets the breaks with little things like judges' decisions on marginal penalties, being able to register late on occasion, judging assignments at the interesting stations, etc.? It is usually the person who has been a help in the past, not a pain. It is usually the person who has been cordial and cooperative with race officials, and who has gone out of his way to say thanks. It is an incredible amount of work to stage a slalom, and it takes so little time and energy to write a brief thank you note or acknowledgment of a job well done. There certainly is no financial reward to be had for organizing a race, so anything racers can do to make the job easier and to encourage the organizer to do it again next year can only benefit everyone.

4

Wildwater Technique

While slalom racing is complicated by artificial obstructions (gates) and unnatural maneuvers (going upstream and backwards), wildwater racing is simpler and more elemental. There is an appealing purity to it; a fast run cannot be demolished by one bizarre gate or a Mr. Magoo gate judge, and, unless you knock the stern off your boat or blow a sprayskirt, you'll finish.

This makes wildwater harsher than slalom; it's less forgiving of weakness in the major factor over which you have control in racing: how hard you are willing to push yourself. If you won the race against the best competition, you worked hard enough. If you lost when you should have won or done better, you can look only to yourself: you didn't work hard enough, probably either in training or in the actual half hour of the race. If you improved, or did better than you expected, or beat some people you'd never beaten before, you will feel justifiably elated—it will be a great thrill and very inspiring.

The slalom racers may be the glamour boys, but wildwater is where character is checked. It is not unlike the difference between Alpine ski racers and cross-country types, who until recently have labored in relative obscurity. And have they labored! But they love it; it's all worth it to them. There must be reasons, just as there are reasons for some of us to specialize in wildwater.

Aside from the stoics who enjoy pain, there are many of us who love wildwater racing for other reasons. Much of it boils down to the belief that we are being challenged continuously at a very high intellectual level; this discipline that seems pure physical labor is actually very challenging to the mind as well. To do well, to improve, we must constantly be thinking, analyzing the stroke, anticipating lines that will lead to the shortest, fastest route. But for the true "student of the stroke," even long flatwater workouts are intellectually challenging, because it takes mental discipline not to be sloppy, to let the stroke get lazy or let the boat wander. To be sure, in order to exercise this discipline the wildwater racer must be in shape, and able to do the requisite work; if your shoulders give out after a couple of hundred strokes and the paddle shaft keeps bouncing off the cockpit rim, no amount of mind control will bring you back to smooth efficiency!

There are other appeals in wildwater racing: the boats are often lovely, always highly specialized race machines. Their single-purpose design is exciting—they are meant to go *fast.* Training can be less complicated—any place you can find a lake, you can get in your boat and go out for a highly useful workout of sprints, intervals or LSD, and it will be as efficient as on your "home" course. There is no need for extra equipment such as the gates, wires, etc., needed by the slalomists. The scenery available to you on long training exercises can also be very attractive, and makes a long workout a very enjoyable session, providing you don't space out on the beauty and forget to concentrate on the task at hand.

Again, we return to the simplicity and purity of the endeavor: your rewards will usually be commensurate with your skills and the quality of your effort in any race, if your goals are reasonably realistic. If you have the minimum talent necessary, you know you can eventually achieve your goals. If you want to make the U.S. Team, you must be prepared to commit everything to that goal, and realize it will take a long time and will include both positive and negative surprises along the way.

Five Factors for Success

Many factors go into making a successful wildwater racer, but we have identified five major physical factors to go along with the mental and emotional discipline discussed above. *Strength* and its importance have been emphasized previously, and must not be overlooked here. *Conditioning* needs more emphasis here than in slalom, because the races are longer and, in slalom, good gate technique and experience can overcome a lack of fitness. In wildwater, if you are not in shape, you will not succeed, either against the competition or against your

own potential. The *forward stroke* is obviously elemental here—you can't win with a lousy stroke, because equally strong, fit, experienced competitors will be more efficient than you and thus faster. *Water reading,* or choosing fast lines and connecting them smoothly, comes with experience and understanding. A racer who looks down the river and doesn't care, or know how to care, where he goes in a rapid, will not find the fast water or the short route, and will work hard with no chance of winning—he will be racing a longer course than his competition! Finally, most major wildwater races are now held on huge water, defined here as fast, very powerful, turbulent streams with big waves, holes and many rocks. Thus, experience, confidence and *big-water ability* are absolutely essential for success at the national and international levels.

In this chapter on wildwater technique we will analyze the final three factors of success (forward stroke, water reading and big-water ability) in detail. For a comprehensive discussion of strength and conditioning, please refer to the chapter on physical conditioning.

The Forward Stroke

To introduce the subject of the forward stroke, let's first take one more step away from the complexity of slalom technique and look at flatwater, Olympic racing. There the variables are reduced even more: straight line, 500 or 1,000 meters, calm water, identical boats, head-to-head competition. In theory, a 2-minute flatwater sprint over 500 meters is done with a few hundred-odd *identical* strokes—no steering, drawing or turning. This is a far cry from the slalomist, who must master a huge repertoire of strokes to serve all sorts of purposes. Somewhere in between, depending on the difficulty of the water, falls the wildwater racer, who steers with leans instead of with a rudder, but who would love to go through a race doing all forward strokes. It doesn't happen, but that's the goal.

Flatwater paddlers spend incredible amounts of time working on their forward stroke—no surprise, given its importance. Scientific, biomechanical scrutiny is now replacing seat-of-the-pants aesthetics in stroke analysis. Wildwater paddlers are getting in the act also, realizing that if they are at home in big water, can learn the course and memorize their lines and can really work hard, their potential is limited only by their technique. Many of them are racing flatwater now, and three major examples come to mind.

Jean-Pierre Burny of Belgium has been World Champion in K-1 wildwater several times, and has competed in several Olympics in flatwater, placing fourth in 1972. Angus Morrison was 1977 U.S. C-1 wildwater champion, after making the Olympic Team in C-1 flatwater for Montreal in 1976. Leslie Klein has been on several U.S. wildwater and flatwater National Teams. It seems the big-water handling skills take a long time to learn, so few notable achievements have yet been made by flatwater racers turning to whitewater (the exception being Andy Toro, many time flatwater Olympian and 1976 U.S. National Champion in C-2 Wildwater). Jean-Pierre, Leslie and Angus have been paddling long enough to have developed fine strokes on top of the prerequisite big-water skills.

A superb forward stroke is best developed on flatwater in a flatwater boat, as demonstrated here by Marcia Smoke. Photo by David Repp.

Flatwater racing is an Olympic sport, with Olympic money. Some of it is spent on training camps, and certainly the ones conducted by Sperry Rademaker in Florida have always encouraged broad participation. Sperry has been a great help to many whitewater paddlers interested in flatwater racing or just in improving their strokes, and is always willing to confer and give advice. Contact her in Floral City, Florida, and make plans to attend a training camp down there. You will receive excellent coaching from those expert in the forward stroke, and it will carry over to whitewater.

To be specific about the forward stroke would require a separate book, because there are many good styles, and a truly in-depth study would be highly technical. We offer a set of fundamentals for both the kayak and canoe strokes, and suggest the only way to build and keep a good stroke is to practice under the watchful eye of a knowledgeable coach or fellow paddler. You can train hard by yourself and still really suffer from having no outside criticism of your stroke. While you are training by yourself, and when you analyze your own or someone else's stroke, think in terms of the concepts below.

Kayak Forward Stroke

The plant. With a slight forward bend at the waist, head up, reach forward and extend the bottom arm, rotating the right shoulder forward, pulling the left shoulder back with the left elbow high and twisting the torso. Drop the blade in right next to the boat with maximum lower arm extension.

The pull and push. Apply power to the blade by untwisting the torso, rotating and pulling back with the right shoulder. At the same time the left arm is straightening and left shoulder is punching forward. Right blade comes back about to your hip (no more), left hand stays to left of center line of boat. Release finger pressure on the shaft with left hand as it punches forward. Exaggerate the body rotation.

A powerful forward stroke propelled Bill Nutt to victory in the 1978 National Wildwater Championships. Photo by Barb McKee.

The exit. Slice the right blade cleanly out of the water by lifting with the right arm, led by the elbow. Try not to drag the back of the blade against the water (now speeding by after your powerful stroke). In the meantime, the left hand and blade are basically waiting, poised to go to the plant on the left side. You now have a full body rotation, right shoulder back, left shoulder forward, heavy emphasis in the stroke on using the powerful torso and back muscles more than the arms.

Repeat on the left.

Additional Concepts:

Good posture. Don't slump, and don't tuck your chin on to your chest—it makes breathing harder.

Pedaling. Push forward with your on-side foot during the stroke, to get your whole body into the rhythm of the motion and help with trunk rotation.

Rhythm. The best paddlers are absolutely beautiful to watch. Their strokes are effortless, and are always smooth and rhythmical, especially on flatwater. To learn good rhythm you must paddle at a medium pace, concentrating on technique and timing. LSD training sessions should lay heavy emphasis on rhythm.

Common Errors

1. Asymmetry—your left side must be the mirror image of your right, with the exception of rotation by the control hand. As an aside, many top paddlers these days are using paddles with the blades offset less than 90°. Even slalom paddlers are using 75° offset blades, making a symmetrical entry and pull much easier, and easing the burden on the wrist of the control hand. Be sure your hands stay equidistant from the blades on both sides, so you aren't favoring one or the other.

Asymmetry can be subtle and happen in many spots. For instance, each paddle blade entry must be identical, as far forward as possible, right next to the boat, with the blade angle the same. The length of the stroke on each side must be the same. The path of the paddle through the water must be straight on each side. The path of the upper hand in the forward push must be the same on each side.

The best help during a stroke technique workout is a video tape machine in the hands of a knowledgeable coach or analyst, which allows you to study your own stroke.

2. Low elbows. Think of how a shot-putter sets up to heave the shot: ball tucked under his chin, elbow out away from his side and up. He can get the maximum push with the elbow and upper arm out at 90° to the torso. The kayak stroke works the same way. Your most efficient and strongest upper-arm position is with the elbow up, pushing forward behind the hand, not from underneath it. You will find the deltoid muscles over the tops of the shoulders do the work in holding the elbows up—they must be conditioned and you must constantly guard against the tendency of the elbows to drop.

3. Short reach. If you lose your concentration you will tend to shorten up your stroke by not making the effort to really twist the torso and reach forward hard with a straight bottom arm at the catch. If you do so, you will lose power drastically and tend to raise your stroke rate to compensate, thus tiring yourself out more quickly. Remember to reach, and to plant the paddle in the water while you have maximum extension, without letting the blade pull back in the air.

4. Death grip. Many paddlers experience cramps in their forearms and hands during races or intense workouts, largely because they are gripping the paddle too hard. Try releasing your fingers from the shaft at the end of the forward push. You must be relaxed to be smooth, and this will help.

5. No rotation. Finally, to emphasize its importance, we mention again the body rotation so necessary for a strong forward stroke. You must twist your torso around your spine as an axis, pushing forward to the catch with the lower shoulder. Then, power is applied through the release of this built-up torque and the flexing of the big muscles of the shoulders, chest and back. No one's arms are strong enough to compete alone against someone else'e entire upper body!

Canoe Forward Stroke

Fundamentally, we all know the canoeist kneels instead of sits, uses a boat that is wider than the kayak, and uses a single-bladed paddle with a T-grip on top. Some of the best canoeists of recent years are also "switchers," equally adept at paddling on either side, and amazingly quick at switching. It seems impossible they don't often end up arcing the paddle toward shore like a twirling baton in the midst of an attempted switch, but they rarely foul up. The best wildwater C-1 paddlers of the future will have to be switchers, because the advantages, especially in very rocky, very technical courses (as in the 1975 World Championships, where switcher Al Button came in third) and in long races are too big to ignore. In any case, there are good canoe strokes, and bad, and once again we will present some fundamentals to be considered in the basic canoe forward stroke.

Most of the principles are the same as in the kayak stroke, in terms of reach, torso rotation, and consistency, but there are three main differences. The one-sided canoeist must steer, he must recover from each stroke by bringing the paddle forward in the air, and he sits 4–8 inches higher off the water than the straight-legged kayaker. These differences will be discussed after we analyze the stroke.

The plant. Instead of lunging forward with the whole torso, which is easy to do with the hips above the level of the cockpit rim, the paddler should go for the long reach by fully extending the bottom arm, twisting the torso around the spine and pushing forward with the lower (on side) shoulder, and pulling back with the top shoulder. This is like coiling a spring, because a powerful torque, ready to unwind, is put into the trunk of the body as it twists away from the paddling side. If the plant occurs at the farthest extension of the reach, a very powerful pull/push will result.

Power. The top arm, which has been cocked slightly at the elbow (elbow high) for the plant, explodes forward in a punch, out and down over the side of the boat as the lower arm pulls back along the side of the boat, with the paddle shaft as vertical as possible. The top hand must push down on the grip, keeping the blade fully submerged—don't bend the top elbow too much, or you will be using the quite weak elbow extension motion to push the paddle grip forward and down. The paddle should enter the water as nearly vertical as possible.

Steering. Logically enough, a C-1 paddled with pure forward strokes on the right will turn lazy circles to the left, since the paddle cannot go down the center line of the boat. This is one major incentive for switching, since steering on one side does not help the forward speed of the boat, while the switcher needs only forward strokes. Steering is accomplished partly by taking advantage of the hull shape of C-1's and leaning away from the stroke (in fact any wildwater boat has a tendency to turn away from a lean). Most steering is done, however, with the paddle, using either the J-stroke or the pry, to counteract the tendency of the stern of the boat to swing to the paddling side. Both strokes push the stern the other way, with the differences being the pry is more powerful and more stable (in that it very quickly can become a low brace) and the J-stroke is much faster. For routine steering in C-1 or C-2 wildwater, you must use a J-stroke.

The J-stroke is hard to teach to a beginner, but is fundamentally sound. It is faster than the pry because there is no transition from pushing the water with one blade face to pushing it with the other, and because usually there is less of a reverse motion, counter to the direction you are going, than there is with the pry. What happens in the J is a smooth continuation of the forward stroke into a kind of hook, where the power face of the blade is pushed out away from the boat. This is accomplished by rolling both wrists out over the shaft in what at first seems an awkward movement but which soon becomes automatic and favored. The J simply steers the boat without slowing it down as much as the pry.

Before leaving the C-boat forward-stroke fundamentals, we should emphasize again the "loading" of the top hand onto the paddle. This is the motion of pushing down hard on the paddle at the catch, thus preventing the tendency of the blade to rise out of the water as it is pulled back before getting perfectly vertical. It makes the fulcrum of the lever be close to the top of the shaft rather than at the bottom hand, which is more powerful and more efficient. It also forces maximum use of the shoulders.

Recovery. While the kayaker gets ready for his next stroke on the right by taking a stroke on the left, the canoeist must quickly bring his one blade forward for another stroke on the same side. The trick here is to be efficient and not be counterproductive, and the key is to keep the top hand high. Whether you do a J at the end of the stroke or not, you should fight the tendency to drop the top hand, thus using the deck over your thigh as a fulcrum. Keep the paddle as upright as possible, and bring it forward, upright, from the exit—don't swing it in a wide, low arc out to the side as with the relaxing cruising stroke, because you will be slower at the catch and you will have created a torque on the boat causing it to try to turn. Similar to swinging a hockey stick in a wide arc while standing on ice, you (and your boat) will tend to counteract the swing by twisting the opposite way. So keep the paddle upright with the blade reasonably close to the boat in the recovery.

Seat Position. While the kayaker sits on or within an inch or two of the hull, the kneeling canoeist has his butt 6–8 inches off the bottom on a thwart or a pedestal. This gives the wildwater canoeist a big advantage in the ability to see ahead and pick good routes, but can make a big difference in stability, especially for guys with heavy upper bodies or fat heads. While the C-1 is wider than the K-1, it has training wheels (called the low brace) on only one side, while the K-1 is covered both ways. You will see many a C-1 paddler falling to his offside, the paddle describing a huge arc over his head in a futile air brace.

The higher seat position gives the canoeist one more advantage: because of the increased leverage available from the higher position, each single stroke should be more powerful than any kayak stroke.

In deciding on seat height, consider comfort, safety and stability. Remember, if you can't stay in your boat for more than half an hour, you will jeopardize your conditioning program. Also, a fast boat or a high seat will do you no good at all if you are so unstable you can't paddle fast and continuously. So the fastest boat for you will inevitably be a compromise, and the leverage given by a high seat may not be useable.

Switching. The three fastest bigwater C-1 wildwater racers we have ever had in this country are switchers—Al Button (3rd in the World in 1975), Angus Morrison (National Champion in 1977 and 1978), and Ben Cass (5th in the World in 1977). Their success lies in their having done it all through their careers, so they really don't have a weak side—they are truly ambidextrous. They are very quick at switching, and thus can do most of their steering with forward strokes. They sometimes switch in awkward situations, and occasionally are susceptible to switching too often, but the advantages clearly outweigh the disadvantages and we would encourage any young canoeists (slalomists too) to do as much learning and paddling on both sides as possible.

Water Reading

Why is it the fellow who usually does well in flatwater workouts can get blown away on the river, especially the unfamiliar river? A major reason could be his inability to find and hold the fastest lines in rapids and between rapids. This is a complicated subject, and one that really cannot be learned except through experience on the river. As you try to gain that experience, think of the following concepts:

1. The deepest water is usually the fastest. Most rapids nearly beg you to follow the best path, since they naturally have a deep, fast channel down the center. Even Evans usually hits those. The problem comes in deciding in marginal situations where there is a tradeoff between the time, distance and effort involved in changing direction to go across the river to seek out such a channel versus the easier, shorter path straight ahead. The final criterion in wildwater is, of course, elapsed time, so you must decide if it is worth it: will you get through this particular rapid faster by going way over there to the fast water? Will you be in the best spot at the end of the rapid to line up for what's ahead? Will you perhaps be faster here, but because of extra energy expended be slower later on? If you stay in the shallow water, do you run the risk of putting a hole in your boat or breaking your paddle? Do you have to run a wicked hole that could cause a capsize?

A wildwater racer in the correct position—just avoiding the big waves. Photo by Bob Woodward.

140

2. Big waves usually mean fast, deep water, but seem to hit awfully hard. At high speed in a wildwater kayak, knifing the bow through a big wave often results in a chest-crushing hit with the body, which not only peels your eyelids back and fouls up your rhythm, it also slows you down! Your best bet is to choose a line down one side or the other of the peaks of the waves, where the water is as fast as in the center but flatter. Just be careful not to cross the eddy line into the slow water. Thus, you must now introduce fine precision into your wildwater technique, because often this line you are seeking is no wider than your boat. You must take that line absolutely flat out, at full speed; you must not use draws and Duffeks and sweeps for your precision, but must use the exact proper entry into the rapid, at the proper angle, with the proper lean, so you can pound through on your best forward strokes without missing a beat.

3. Short cuts may be faster, but surely are in slower water. A river with sharp curves in it presents the problem of whether to cut off the corner by going to the inside in the (usually) slower water. To the outside the water is faster, but your goal is the fastest time, not pure boat speed. So the answer is obvious: if you get through the corner faster by cutting inside, do it. Now try to figure in the risk of putting a hole in the boat in the shallows, the position you will be in at the bottom to line up for the next rapid, the difficulty of the approach, and you will have your answer.

4. Scan the river ahead, sometimes from the bottom up. Ca-

Ouch! A momentum-stopping wave catches a wildwater racer in the face. This boater should have been able to avoid this wave.

noeists should take advantage of their ability to see ahead from their exalted position, and read the rapids as far downstream as possible. In fact, it is often best to figure the line through a rapid from the bottom up, figuring where the fast water exits the rapid, then following the best path back up to the entry. Sometimes this method will cause you to take what appears to be an inferior approach into a rapid, but will reap rewards of speed and position downstream. Regardless, just as the driver of a car cruising along at 55 must look way ahead, so, too, the wildwater racer finds that to concentrate on the rocks going by is to miss opportunities to pick good lines from enough distance to make good use of them.

Big Water Ability

The outstanding young paddlers that have emerged out of the Washington, D.C. area in recent years have many things going for them, most of which have been discussed earlier. They have been successful in all kinds of races, from pool slaloms to flooded World Championship courses. One of their distinguishing features is their complete cool in big water. Not only do they train and play on the Potomac, which can be awesome and incredibly difficult in places, but they have raced in every big-water race in the country. By now, they have become remarkably at ease and controlled in big water, with absolute confidence in their rolls and the knowledge borne of experience that they can handle anything.

This competence is no accident, and yet gaining it can be one of the pure joys of whitewater paddling—it is a classic case of learning while playing. And we mean out-and-out, pure play—laughing, hot-dogging, showing-off, doing absolutely outrageous stunts. The usual goal here is the perfect, airborne, waving ender. This is a deliberate attempt to bury the nose of the boat in the trough of a big wave or hole, so when the paddler's weight is thrown forward the bow will sink and the stern will be thrown sky high, up and over. Perfect enders are rare, but even dramatic endstands (glorified pop-ups) are given no credit unless the paddler waves, either to his buddies or, better yet, to the camera. Creativity in ender contests is rewarded as well; exceptional effort shown by waving with both hands after having thrown the paddle away is applauded warmly. Of course, no ender, no matter how straight over, no matter how much air time there is, counts at all if the paddler swims. Doing enders, actually all playing in big water, requires three major attributes: courage, a bomb-proof roll and a strong boat.

All three of these relate to confidence in one way or another, and it should be obvious lots of playing in big water will have an enormous impact on a paddler's confidence level, which translates *directly* to the race. While their opponents are perspiring at the thought of the tough ferry move across the huge wave in the middle of the slalom course, the D.C. kids and others comfortable in big water are planning the moves for the gates and wondering if they could get an ender in, with the big crowd watching, and still make the next gate!

It works the same way in wildwater—the world's best racers can *race* in huge water, not merely survive. They are so strong, so comfortable, so confident in the big waves, holes and boulder gardens, they seem to be paddling on the lake as they go flying by. No braces, back strokes or obvious steering strokes. They can pick their lines and hold them as well in the monstrous stuff as in the ripples, and, of course, their superiority is demonstrated more convincingly in this type of water than in easy water, because they have control of the major new variable.

The lesson for all of us is clear: to be a successful international racer, you must be at home in big water. You must relish it. The only way to get comfortable in it is to play in it often, pushing yourself to try crazy things, being willing (and able!) to roll almost anywhere, commanding the scene rather than being pushed around out of control. This is where whitewater training is most fun, because we are demanding, indeed ordering, you spend some days in pure, hell-raising, exhausting play!

Flatwater Paddling

Training for wildwater racing has to include many miles of flatwater work, for two reasons: it is the best place to work on stroke technique, and it is the best place for really rigorous conditioning workouts with sprints, intervals or distance work.

Flatwater is essential for stroke work because the variables are reduced enough to allow you to concentrate exclusively on technique. Your coach, partner, fellow paddlers, and/or the video tape machine can all help with your stroke, and, in a 5–10 mile LSD workout, you can get into a rhythm and concentrate on nothing but the proper stroke. For a complete discussion on types of workouts, please refer to the chapter on physical conditioning.

A Month-Long Plan for a Big Race

Let's assume you are training for the wildwater Nationals a month away on the Savage River, a difficult, fast, very cold Class IV run that will take 22–26 minutes, depending on the class. Assuming also you have built a good base with a year-round weight training program and have put in lots of miles in the boat in previous months, how should you go about assuring your best possible performance a month from now? For a year-long training plan, look over the training schedule provided in the chapter on physical conditioning.

First, create a training schedule with a calendar in front of you, being realistic about things you must do other than training: your sister's wedding, exams, moving from school to home, graduation, etc. Then plan the races you feel you should attend—in general, as many as possible without killing yourself with half a dozen full-day drives to and from races. Note where you will be and what training facilities you will have available at each place. Then schedule each day, the plan being to peak physically, emotionally, and mentally in 30 days.

Let's look at a possible schedule, with the following assumptions: you are living at home the whole time, have two hours a day to train, have two available races before the Nationals, you live six hours from the Savage, you have never paddled there before, you have only flatwater on which to train in the boat, and you have access to a good universal gym.

Before you go any further, determine if there will be any releases on the Savage in advance of race weekend so you can take some practice runs. Since you have never run the Savage, you will be at a great disadvantage until it becomes familiar to you and you can race hard on it without worrying about what's around the bend. The Savage is managed for flood control purposes, and rarely releases water under ordinary weather conditions unless there is a special request for a major race by the ACA. Find out from the race organizer if any releases are planned in the next month, and, if there are, give a high priority to taking as many runs as possible on the course.

Plan your equipment needs. Is the boat you have now going to be O.K. for the race? If you need a new boat, do you have the money, or time and ability to get used to it before the race? Is your paddle old and cracking? You must pay attention to your equipment, so that on race day you are so confident that it is a positive factor, not a real or potential hassle.

Schedule

The race is Saturday, day 28.

Sunday, day 1. Long intervals on the lake, with a total of 60–75 minutes of "power on." This will be a long workout, but it's Sunday, and you have the time.

Monday, day 2. An hour in the boat; steady paddling that produces a pulse of 130–140 bpm (beats per minute) throughout the workout. Later, a maintenance weight workout, one of seven scheduled in the next four weeks.

Tuesday, day 3. A short, intense, maximum effort, boat workout, doing starts from a dead stop with maximum output. Go for 20–30 seconds, rest as long as it takes to stop the boat, but no more than 10–15 seconds. Do three sets of 10 repetitions, with three minutes between sets.

Wednesday, day 4. A long, medium-effort, conditioning and technique workout. Try to put your stroke back together after yesterday's thrashing. This could be a 10-mile paddle emphasizing rhythm and good stroke, ending with a push in the last mile that keeps your pulse above 150.

Thursday, day 5. Perhaps a foot run, or an easy boat workout, followed by a good weight session.

Friday, day 6. Off, with a three-hour drive to a race. Try to get a good night's sleep.

Saturday, day 7. A slalom race, for variety, fun and because you like slalom. Don't loaf, and before or after the slalom, make several runs on the wildwater course for tomorrow's race.

Sunday, day 8. Wildwater race, medium difficulty. Realizing you are tired and not peaking, do your best. Remember, this race is a means to an end as well as an end in itself. Try to win, but also use the race as a stepping stone to the Nationals. Control your psyche factor so that you work hard without spending yourself emotionally—you should be eager for a workout the next day.

Monday, day 9. You are probably tired after the race weekend, but use this as a test: what kind of mental discipline can you force on yourself when you're tired and don't feel like getting in the boat? Force yourself to paddle with your absolute best stroke, and once you get the bugs out, go ahead and do a tough workout: pyramid intervals, with a total of 20–30 minutes on.

Tuesday, day 10. Stay out of the boat, but do a good weight workout. Get psyched for tomorrow's monster.

Wednesday, day 11. This should be a real heavy workout, with a 2–3 mile warmup, then many long intervals (3–4 minutes), with enough rest in between to let the pulse drop to 110 or 120. Pyramid: 2 min., rest, 2½, rest, 3, rest, 3½, rest, 4, rest, 3½, rest, 3, rest, 2½, rest, 2. Then rest 5 minutes, and repeat it. That will be 52 minutes on. Then coax yourself to grunt out 10 x 30 strokes, all-out sprints.

Thursday, day 12. Off!

Friday, day 13. Lift weights, then do a 30–60-minute technique session at 120-130 bpm. Maybe 5 miles.

Saturday, day 14. The big race is 2 weeks away, and you should reach your workout peak in 8–10 days (Mon. or Tues. day 23 or 24). If the Savage is running, go to it and get in as many runs as possible. If it is not, maybe use the freedom of the weekend to run a big-water river if there is one available, several times in your wildwater boat if possible. For variety's sake, consider leaving the race boat at home and going off to play in your cruising boat in your favorite stream. Be careful of too much driving, because you have races each of the next two weekends. If you want to stay at home and keep plugging it out in the boat, try a race simulation: time yourself over a distance on your lake that takes approximately 30 minutes.

Sunday, day 15. Push yourself through another hard boat workout doing 30–40 minutes on in an interval workout.

Monday, day 16. Stay out of the boat. Foot run several miles, then do your fifth weight workout for strength maintenance. Don't kill yourself.

Tuesday, day 17. If possible, do a tough slalom workout! If not, do a 10-miler with a fast last mile.

Wednesday, day 18. Heavy intervals again, with two workouts today if possible. (Obviously, if you have time, two workouts 4 or 5 days a week are excellent.)

Thursday, day 19. Your sixth weight workout, with a hard paddle at the opposite end of the day. Race your measured distance on the lake again.

Friday, day 20. Rest day. Drive

to your second pre-Nationals race. Try to sleep well tonight, for Sunday's race.

Saturday, day 21. Put a priority on running the wildwater course in your WW boat instead of racing in the slalom. Do both if possible, but remember that if you race slalom you'll probably have a time-consuming work assignment as well. You need time in your wildwater boat in wildwater! It would be good psychologically if you could do well in tomorrow's race, so don't fag yourself out completely today.

Sunday, day 22. With the Nationals six days away, you should be getting really psyched. Expend some of that energy today in the race by putting out a maximum effort. Blow yourself out, remembering again, this race is a means as well as an end. Your mind and emotions are still focused on next Saturday.

Monday, day 23. A good, solid weight workout today, together with a medium foot run of 3–5 miles. Also, get all your logistical ducks in a row for the weekend: boat and other equipment repair, travel plans, car maintenance, lodging plans, eating plans, victory celebration plans, etc.

Tuesday, day 24. This should be your real bomber workout: 2–3 miles warmup, with good technique and no loafing. Then 30 x 30 second standing start sprints, then two interval pyramids with 4 to 6 minutes in each at half-minute increments. Sleep well. (If your previous weekend's wildwater race was Saturday instead of Sunday and you thus got home a day earlier, this heavy workout should be done on Monday, day 23).

Wednesday, day 25. You are now beginning recovery to your peak in four days. This and the next two days should be rebuilding days, allowing stressed, fatigued tissues, muscles and minds to rejuvenate. So today either don't paddle at all or do a couple of loafing miles. Don't get sloppy, but keep your pulse under 110. Be sure to rest well and often, and get a good night's sleep.

Thursday, day 26. Again, a light loosening up workout in the boat for a few miles. Sleep well.

Friday, day 27. If you did not drive to the Savage yesterday, you will do it today and it should be early, if possible. The water will probably be on for a couple of hours, so take two runs if you can.

Saturday, day 28. This is it! If the water is on early enough, you might consider taking another familiarization run. There is real risk, though, in possible damage to equipment that may require fiberglass repair right before the race, if indeed there is enough time at all. Be careful.

For the race itself, you must be relaxed and loose, yet ready to max yourself out. If will be over before you know it, and your mid-race fatigue will seem like nothing if you lose the race by two seconds knowing you could have gone harder.

Warm Up

We suggest you warm up for the race in the boat, if possible. Running an easy section of the river could do it, or paddling on the nearby lake. (If it's very cold and wet, be certain you can get warm and dry after the warm up.) This is an hour or two before your start, and, of course, must be followed with an in-the-boat warm up above the starting line. Get your heart going, get the blood pumped to the muscles, get them warm, and don't worry about tiring yourself out in the warm up. You are in good shape. Think about your lines, and try to be relaxed and loose.

The Start

The exact minute of your start will be published in advance, so you have no excuses for not having yourself ready in every way. (Number on, good spray skirt, etc.) The start will be at minute intervals, and you will find it incredibly exciting yet low-key. As you sit in the warm-up area watching others go off, don't change your strategy or be psyched out by their starts. As you move into the starter's hold, get ready! Stay loose, but be alert and ready to go on one, because the boat won't start moving until GO! Don't start out frantically, but quickly and powerfully.

During the Race

Most importantly, you must race intelligently, and you must work hard. This requires intense concentration; you are studying the water near you at the same time as you are watching the water a minute or two ahead. You must avoid positional surprises, so you don't come into a rapid on the wrong side because you did not recognize where you were. You must give yourself lots of clues along the way, so you know where you are and what's ahead. We have found it useful to give names to as many of the rapids as possible, then to work on knowing their sequence. This can really help when you are fatigued and could possibly get confused. You will be surprised at how similar many places on a river can look.

The middle section of the race is where mental discipline is the telling factor, since most people can start quickly and many can sprint with the finish line in sight. But, a fast last quarter mile, in which you can gain at most 5–10 seconds, does little good if you let 30 seconds get away in the middle of the race. So, try not to let down 8–15 minutes into the race. Try to keep up the stroke rate, keep pulling hard, in order to be in it when the final minutes approach. The classic coach's line to the 12th place finisher who is in a frantic sprint at the finish line is "if you have that much left, you did not paddle the rest of the race hard enough."

The Finish

Having said all that about really killing yourself in the middle of the race, we now emphasize how important it is to really go for it at the end. Many, many races have been decided by less than one second, and in 1978 there was a tie, to the tenth of a second, for second place in the C-2 Wildwater class at the National Championships. Of course, all four guys were kicking themselves at the end.

In 1969, the C-1 wildwater race was over 40 minutes long. If the 7th-place finisher had been four seconds faster he would have been fourth; four seconds slower, 11th. Don't save yourself for the final sprint, but use everything you've got when it comes time. After you finish, warm down gradually with a few minutes of easy paddling.

Recovery

Did you win? Did you place? Did you do as well as you had hoped? As you wind down, drive home, and begin preparations for the next race, try to analyze the results and your own performance so you can get the most out of them. Look back at the race and your preparation for it in reference to all the concepts and suggestions made in this chapter. Ask the right questions, then seek the necessary improvements. Were you fit enough? Did your technique deteriorate badly? Did you push yourself hard enough? Was your boat dry at the end? Was your water reading good? Did you know the river well enough? Were your lines good in the rapids?

If you can train as much and as hard as suggested by the month-long preparation calendar provided earlier, it shouldn't be very long before you are competing at the top.

Splits

It is usually possible at one or more points in a wildwater race to set up "splits" and have them called out to the racers. This allows a paddler, basically alone on the river, to know where he stands relative to a boat ahead of him. The ability to provide splits depends on the fact that there is a very precise, known interval between boats—usually one minute.

The technique is quite simple in theory, often confusing and troublesome in practice. The split taker finds out from his friend Joe whom he would like splits off of—let's say Bill, who starts 8 minutes ahead. The split taker must note on his wristwatch the exact second that Bill goes by his checkpoint, which should be some ways upstream and easily visible (to give computation and communication time). If Joe is tied with him, he will come by exactly 8 minutes later. If Joe appears in 7:40, he is 20 seconds ahead; if he arrives in 9:01, he is 61 seconds down. The split taker should bellow, loudly and clearly, the exact information: "You're 20 seconds up!" or "You're 61 seconds down!" The information is supposed to be an incentive, a psych up, that can be used by the paddler for the rest of the race.

Training Partners

Training alone can be a drag, and often is not as productive as training in pairs or groups. If at all possible, try to train with mates of similar aspirations and abilities, or better yet, helpful folks who are better or faster than you. Your workouts will be more rigorous and consistent, and more fun by a long shot! You will be able to push each other, and to prevent lapses and laziness that are really hard to guard against when you are alone. Of course, you must race alone, so don't ignore the development of the discipline you will need when race day comes.

5

Physical Preparation

Slalom and wildwater racing require significant amounts of strength, speed/quickness, and stamina, with slalom requiring more strength and quickness and wildwater demanding more stamina. Acquiring these qualities is the most talked about, publicized, and easily measurable aspect of training and racing. Whenever racers gather the discussion usually turns to physical training.

The underlying thought of your training program should be: will the training you are doing enable you to move your boat faster and more precisely than you can now? We believe your physical training must be "specific," that is, as much as possible, you must do exercises that simulate paddling motions and use paddling muscles. All the weights lifted, sprints endured, and miles run are but means to the ultimate end of making your boat go faster and more exactly where you want it during a race. You must be sure your physical training program is directed toward specifically appropriate strength and endurance development.

Through physical training you are trying to make your body more efficient in order to utilize your skill and technique. Physiologically, this means you want to develop an efficient cardiovascular system (heart, lungs, and the distribution system for fuel and oxygen to the muscles). You want to make the muscles involved in paddling stronger for rapid initial movement of the boat. Slalom demands quick acceleration and constant changes in pace. Wildwater racing is more of a constant, cyclical motion required over 20–30 minutes. Although much of the training for the two disciplines may be similar, the unique aspects of each demand different approaches in training.

In this chapter, we will look first at recent developments resulting from the physiological testing done on members of the Eastern Whitewater Team, which has given us our first in-depth understanding of cardiovascular efficiency and how to develop it through training. Following this will be a discussion of the various training methods used in both on-the-water and off-the-water training, with a thorough discussion on strength training. Then all of the factors involved will be brought together with a sample month-by-month training plan leading up to the big race of the year. The chapter will close with a look at diet, drugs, and common physical problems.

Physiological Testing with Dave Pendergast

In recent years members of the Eastern Whitewater Team have undergone extensive physical testing at the University of New York at Buffalo under the direction of Dr. Dave Pendergast, a physiologist who has done similar testing with athletes in a broad spectrum of sports.

These tests mark the first time that paddlers have been able to analyze objectively their physical status and to plan training programs based on their personal strengths and weaknesses. Doing justice in explaining Pendergast's testing program would demand a book in itself. However, the most salient points can be brought to light here.

Aerobic Power and Anaerobic Capacity

Several concepts must be defined at the outset of this discussion. Both slalom and wildwater racing require "aerobic power" and a certain amount of "anaerobic capacity." The amount of aerobic power one has refers to the ability to work (exercise) at a high rate while supplying all the oxygen the working muscles need at the time of the exertion. Anaerobic capacity refers to the ability to work at a rate so intense that the athlete is not able to meet the oxygen demands of the working muscles. He therefore builds up an oxygen debt which must be repaid at the end of the exertion. Thus, a marathon is run almost entirely aerobically, while a 100-meter or even a 400-meter dash is run almost entirely anaerobically. A racer can paddle at an anaerobic level for just a minute or so; at the end of that time he will either cease paddling or will have to decrease the pace and drop back to an aerobic level.

A 20-minute wildwater race will demand that a racer paddle at an aerobic level for much of the race, and the racer will only go into an anaerobic state in the final mad minute or so leading to the finish, after which he can repay his oxygen debt. A slalom paddler, in a 4-minute course, will also race at an aerobic level for much of the race, dipping into his anaerobic reserves upon occasion down the course and at the finish.

The Central and Peripheral Cardiovascular Systems

Two cardiovascular systems are at work during training and racing. For the sake of the discussion here, let's define them in laymen's terms as the central and peripheral systems. The central system is the heart, lungs, and major arteries. The peripheral system consists of the other arteries, arterioles, and capillaries of the working muscles; with paddlers this would include the arms, shoulders, and other upper body muscles used while paddling.

The central system takes in oxygen and delivers it to the peripheral system. The peripheral system then uses what is given to it by the central system to keep the muscles working at a high rate.

The most efficient way to develop the central system (and certainly the simplest) is by hard, aerobic running, because running involves large muscle masses. The central system can also be developed by hard, aerobic paddling, but not nearly so efficiently—the arms and shoulders at a full work level simply do not place as much demand on the central system as do the legs at a full work level. Conversely, by far the best way to develop the peripheral paddling system is by paddling at a hard, aerobic level.

Physiological testing at SUNY (Buffalo). Dave Pendergast and his assistant stand on the movable platform which will rotate around the circular water tank at whichever speed the paddler can maintain. Photo by SUNY (Buffalo).

The Testing Procedures

Various tests were conducted on the paddlers to measure their physical condition, their aerobic power, and their anaerobic capacity:

1. Total submersion in a water tank to determine percentage of body fat. Most of the top male paddlers measured between 6 and 10 percent with the female paddlers recording slightly higher figures.

2. Running on a treadmill to determine the athlete's maximum oxygen uptake, a measure of aerobic power. Samples of exhaled air were taken at intervals. Brent Turner recorded the highest figures with 85 milliliters of oxygen per li-

Leslie Klein paddles while samples of her exhaled air are collected during physiological testing at SUNY (Buffalo). Photo by SUNY (Buffalo).

ter of air per kilogram of body weight. Many paddlers were in the 60's and 70's.

3. In-the-boat testing with air bags to determine aerobic power while paddling.

4. Blood lactate samples taken from the arm after paddling to maximum, to help measure anaerobic capacity.

5. Arm cranking on a machine to measure the aerobic power of only the arms (rest of the upper body kept immobile).

What the Tests Showed

Through two days of testing in Buffalo, paddlers could see very clearly where they were strong, where they were weak, and what exercise program would be most appropriate for improving the weak areas. Some folks had relatively well developed central systems, but had inefficient peripheral systems, so that their muscles could not use all of the oxygen and fuel that could be delivered. Such people need work on explosive muscle power and raw speed; for them, a combination of weight training and paddling at a high, aerobic level would be best.

Other paddlers had well developed peripheral systems which were capable of utilizing more oxygen than their relatively weak central systems could deliver. Crucial to improvement for these folks is a training regimen to develop aerobic power. They were told to go out and run, if they wanted to go faster in the boat!

Remember that the athletes we are describing are veterans and are at the top of the sport in every sense: strength, conditioning, technique, experience. While it is always useful to have information about ourselves to help us work on areas that are weak, early in your racing career it is probably safe to say that the area that needs the most work is technique. Therefore, be careful of "wasting" a lot of your precious training time by running, lifting weights, swimming, doing calisthenics, etc.; you would probably be better advised to spend as much time in the boat in gates and/or on the river as you possibly can, working on the infinite possibilities you must master from the technical standpoint. Only when you cannot be in your boat, or when you need a break, should you spend a lot of time on other phases of training. When technique becomes less of a limiting factor, and you begin squandering clean runs because you run out of gas at gate 13, then you must incorporate more physical training and conditioning into your schedule.

Summary

1. Realizing that technique overrides all other concerns in racing success, it is important to note that the most dominant *physical* factor involved is aerobic power, for both wildwater and slalom. Aerobic power is best developed by running (or cross-country skiing) and hard distance paddling at an intensity of at least 85% of race pace. In the past, most paddlers have done their distance work at too slow a pace, thereby deriving little aerobic benefit.

2. Anaerobic capacity can be developed to its maximum during the season with six weeks of anaerobic training. Therefore, the last six weeks of training leading up to the big race or the first of a big series of races should see a combination of aerobic and anaerobic training. Prior to that six-week period, the emphasis should be on developing aerobic power. Once you work through the six-week period, you can maintain your anaerobic maximum with continued anaerobic workouts.

3. It takes an athlete longer to recover from anaerobic training than from aerobic training. Since the theory behind conditioning is to stress the appropriate muscles and then have them recover to a point where they are stronger than before the stress, it makes sense to allow time for recovery between anaerobic workouts. (In fact, it is mandatory for optimum results.) Paddlers doing heavy anaerobic work twice a day, or even once a day for days on end, are either not doing the anaerobic work with enough intensity or are not allowing time for proper recovery between sessions and are inviting chronic fatigue.

4. Many racers, reared on interval workouts twice a day during the spring and pushed by the impatience and excitement surrounding the first races after a long winter, reach their physical peak in April or May and do not improve later in the summer for the really important races. They usually would be better off to plan their year more carefully, postponing the emphasis on interval sessions until later in the year leading up to the big races. Later in this chapter we will look at how to plan your training schedule for the entire year and will also mention some examples from recent seasons.

5. Finally, remember that here we are talking about physical factors, not slalom or wildwater technique. Dedicated slalom racers know that two and sometimes three workouts a day are necessary in mid-season to work on and sharpen technique, and that a good part of their technique training should be done at high speed. Therefore, racers must balance the need for a large quantity of technique work with the physical impact this will have on aerobic power, anaerobic capacity, and fatigue.

The Warm Up and the Warm Down

Before discussing specific workouts both on and off the water, the value of a proper warm-up and warm-down should be mentioned. In order to prevent injury and to enable the working muscles to obtain maximum benefit from a workout, it is vital that you engage in at least 10 minutes of warming up prior to a workout. This means 10 minutes of stretching and working of the muscles which will be stressed during the workout. Upon finishing the workout, allow for 10 minutes of gradual warming down in order to facilitate waste removal from the working muscles.

In order to develop and maintain flexibility, help prevent muscle and tendon strain, and rid the muscles of waste products accumulated during a training session, 5–10 minutes of stretching each day following a workout will do wonders. While stretching, keep in mind:

1. Hold a slight, easy stretch for 15–30 seconds and then gradually increase it.
2. Do not stretch to the point of discomfort.
3. Proper stretching is done without bouncing.

On-the-Water Training

There are as many ways to make a body adapt to the demands of racing as there are racers. Everyone has his own way of training and each person's program is constantly undergoing revision as new methods are discovered and found beneficial. Although the definition of terms and types of training will remain constant during the discussion of both on-the-water and dry-land workouts, it will be the skillful way in which you combine and emphasize those aspects of training most applicable to you which will determine your success. Your program will, of course, vary from another paddler's according to limitations of time, location, facilities, commitment and personal strengths and weaknesses.

The best method of training for paddling is paddling. You can't get more specific than that. There are various ways of training to develop endurance and speed and these common forms can be used by both slalom and wildwater paddlers. These forms of training are distance, fartlek, interval and sprint training. When used alone, or better yet, in combination, these training methods will condition the cardiovascular, muscular and respiratory systems specifically to improve racing performance.

Distance

Long distance training is a basic and favorite method, especially in the off-season and early season, to build stamina and work on technique. A steady, uniform pace should be continued throughout the training session. Remembering what was brought to light with the Buffalo testing, for maximum results you should paddle at or near 85% of race pace. Use a talk test; if you can carry on a conversation with a training partner during a distance workout, you're not putting in enough effort.

Distance paddling is the best way

Distance workouts may be done in a flatwater boat. Photo by Kerry Cox.

of building aerobic power, and while distance training develops endurance in terms of cardiac efficiency more slowly than does interval training, the endurance attained is more stable and long lasting. A good distance workout lasts at least an hour, with many of today's wildwater paddlers covering at least eight miles during a distance session.

Fartlek

Fartlek is a famous Swedish training method originally used by runners. It is translated as "speed play." Fartlek is a system of untimed endurance training with hard paddling alternated with periods of easy paddling, race speed bursts and all-out sprints. The emphasis is on total paddling time rather than on a number of exact distances, exact times and exact recovery periods. The main quality developed by fartlek is stamina. But it also develops some speed, depending on how much speed work is introduced into the training session.

Fartlek training can be continued for a hour or two, and this fast-slow paddling should be used extensively during the early season. A possible example of a fartlek training session would be to paddle slowly for about five minutes, paddle 1000 meters at a good clip, go back to five minutes of slow paddling and then throw in a short, hard burst. The possibilities are endless. Doing "leap frogs," in which you pass and are re-passed by your training partner during a wildwater run or distance session, is a form of fartlek.

Interval

Interval training consists of paddling a series of repeat efforts over a given distance or time with a controlled amount of rest between efforts. Important factors in a proper interval training session are: the distance to be repeated, the number of times the distance is paddled, the pace at which the distance is paddled and the recovery interval of relaxed paddling. With this system you can do an almost infinite variety of workouts.

In interval training the greatest cardiovascular improvement occurs during the recovery phase when the heart rate is being reduced from approximately 180 to 120 bpm (beats per minute). The greatest amount of blood pumped per heart beat is during the interval of rest immediately following the exertion. Since endurance is related to the amount of blood the heart can pump in a given period, interval training produces the best endurance results in the shortest time.

However, keep in mind that distance training followed by interval training will produce the most long-lasting peak of endurance, much more so than just interval training alone. Many whitewater athletes abuse interval training, feeling that all of the work periods during an interval workout have to be all-out efforts. In introducing intervals to your training program after an early season devoted to distance and fartlek, you will want to make them more endurance-oriented than speed-oriented. This means doing a longer period of work at less than full effort combined with a rather short and not quite complete rest period. As the season progresses, the shift should be to shorter, more intense work periods punctuated with rest periods allowing more complete recovery.

Here are two examples of interval workouts, one which you would do early in the spring and one later during the racing season.

April Interval Session: 90 seconds "on" at race speed followed by 60 seconds "off" of relaxed paddling. Repeat 10 times, rest five minutes, then repeat the process.

June Interval Session: 30 seconds on at 95% full sprint followed by 60 seconds of relaxed paddling. Repeat eight times, rest five minutes, do it again, rest again, then do it a third time.

If the emphasis is on building endurance, then the work period should be long and the rest interval short. If the emphasis is on building speed and quickness, the work period should be short and intense and the rest interval should be longer.

Sprints

Sprint training is the final refinement of interval training and consists of paddling all-out efforts at top sprinting speed. Top speed cannot be maintained for more than 30–35 seconds in a kayak or canoe.

There should be a relatively long rest period between each all-out sprint. Your breathing should return to normal and your heart rate should be below 100 bpm. In an all-out sprint, you are not able to take in oxygen as fast as it is used, with the result that you build up an oxygen debt which must be repaid during the rest interval. Sprinting adapts the body to tolerate high levels of oxygen debt while distance work, at the other end of the spectrum, adapts the body to absorb large quantities of oxygen while paddling. Sprint training, along with most forms of interval training, is anaerobic in nature, and in six weeks you will develop your anaerobic capacity to its maximum for that season. The emphasis on sprint training should come in the weeks prior to the big race of the season.

For flatwater conditioning work, we prefer to use a wildwater boat instead of a slalom boat. Pushing a slalom boat at full speed on flatwater is no fun, although in the few weeks leading up to a big race, all your work should be done in a slalom boat if you are a slalom paddler so that total boat familiarity is achieved.

If you can do the above types of training on whitewater so much the better. Most people are limited to flatwater workouts throughout most of the year, but don't miss the whitewater opportunities when they present themselves.

Slalom Gate Sequences

While slalom paddlers can also benefit from flatwater paddling with the wildwater racers, especially in the off-season when acquiring aerobic power is of prime importance, the favorite method of training for slalom paddlers involves running gate sequences either on flat or whitewater. If the gates are on whitewater, try to set the gates so that you can paddle back up to the start after each sequence. Sequences of gates can be long or short, fast or slow, depending on your objectives for that workout. Early in the season, it might be wise to practice long, slow sequences, concentrating on technique. In the middle of the racing season, the sequences can be short, very fast bursts of 20–60 seconds. Penalties should be watched carefully in all gate work. Some people say that all-out sprinting through the gates without worrying about hitting the poles has its place, but you can go almost as fast and still make that extra mental and physical effort not to hit the poles. Before big races, long, high-speed timed and scored sequences will prepare you best.

One popular workout consists of having two or three kayaks in the water doing a sequence while someone on shore does the timing. The rest interval for each boater occurs as he paddles to the start. Each run is timed and scored, yet the paddler does not get his time announced if he touches a pole. Only those with clean runs have their times given to them.

Keep in mind that slow, sustained gate work is an aerobic workout, while hard, race-speed efforts qualify as interval work or sprint work and the same emphasis on proper rest and recovery between sessions should be observed.

Indoor Pool Training

For those boaters living in the northern reaches of the country where outdoor paddling in the winter is impossible, indoor pool training has become an accepted and popular form of refining techniques and maintaining the fitness of specific kayak/canoe muscles. Pool training, unlike outdoor practice on a river, requires efficient use of a limited body of water, usually by a large group of people with limited time. The trick is to discover basic training techniques which require very little water space but which at the same time simulate outdoor water conditions.

Wildwater paddlers can make use of a paddle board or rack. A paddle board consists of two wooden 2x4's connected by cross pieces, as in a ladder. You can fit a molded kayak seat in the middle and have an adjustable foot brace and/or outfit the rack for C boats. Place a full-length mirror in front of you on the pool deck to watch your forward stroke. With a paddle board, you sit in the seat, paddle, yet do not move. Don't try this with a normal-size blade as the water resistance will be too great. Shave the blades down (3″ wide) to simulate the water resistance you will encounter in moving water.

Slalom paddlers can hang gates and, in a 25-meter pool, a group of five gates is usually employed; one in each corner of the pool and one in the middle. English Gates (a series of standard maneuvers in and around a single gate) can be done as well as gate sequences. By starting a couple of boats only 10 sec-

A rear view of the paddleboard. Note the mirror in the front.

Leslie Klein and Terry White work on the paddleboard indoors during the winter of 1979.

onds apart, it is possible to maintain two boaters on the course at the same time. Those waiting their turn in line can do the timing for those who are on the course. The sequential route should be changed or redesigned after each boater has had 5–7 runs over the course. To add a little spice, include an Eskimo Roll or two.

The following is a description of one of the pool workouts Eric did five mornings a week in winter training. The crucial thing to remember is that he was alone in the pool with someone timing him. He had the basic arrangement of a gate in each of the corners and one in the middle of the pool. Some terms need defining:

1. A whistle drill is a timed, all-out effort through the outside four gates. When the timer blew once on the whistle, Eric would turn, changing from paddling forward to paddling backward, yet continuing in the same direction. Two blows on the whistle and Eric immediately headed in the opposite direction. Only the timer knew when he was going to blow the whistle. It's a great exercise for slalom—lots of stopping and starting. After each whistle drill, the pulse was taken (the PR under Score).

2. A double or triple run refers to a sequence of gates done two or three times in a row.

3. Of course, all penalties for the entire hour were accounted for.

4. Jay's Surprise was a different exercise each morning.

Exercise	Penalties	Score (In Seconds)
10 Minute Warm Up		
2 Minute Whistle Drill	10	PR 168
40 Second Rest		
1st Sequence Practice Run		
1st double run	10	100.8
1st triple run	20	155.8
2nd double run	10	99.8
Single English Gate	0	59.0
40 Second Rest		
3 Minute Whistle Drill	20	PR 180
40 Second Rest		
2nd Sequence Practice Run		
1st double run	20	107.9
1st triple run	0	165.2
2nd double run	0	108.2
1 Minute Whistle Drill	0	PR 160
40 Second Rest		
Double English Gate	0	122.9
40 Second Rest		
4 Minute Whistle Drill	10	PR 180
40 Second Rest		
Jay's Surprise—6 Forward Sprints	—	
Total Penalties	100	

Off-the-Water Training

Strength Training

So much has been written in recent years about the importance of muscle power in sports that we want to give you a thorough understanding of the current "state of the art" as it relates to paddling. As background, two major changes in conventional thinking have occurred which are worth noting.

First, strength training is now universally accepted as a key ingredient in nearly every sport, including those once thought to be exempt. Swimming is the best example, where the exceptionally powerful East German women literally burst on the scene in 1973, garnering *every* world record, with a significant amount of weight training behind them. It had been thought that weight lifting caused *bulk* and *inflexibility,* both anathema to the sleek swimmer's needs; the East Germans were willing to add some size to their muscles to get the accompanying strength, and at the same time designed their exercises to incorporate lots of stretching and exercising through a full range of motion, thereby increasing their flexibility. Strength allows strokes to move the body faster through the water; in other sports, it was realized that we could jump higher, kick farther, throw more accurately and, in general, be more in control, with greater strength.

Second, in nearly all sports in which they compete at a national or international level, women now use strength training. At most universities 5–7 years ago there was nary a female within a mile of the weight room; these days, many just put the nose clips on and endure the place with the rest of us. The stigma and the embarrassment are gone, and the old worry about grotesque body shapes is largely gone, as women have found regular strength training often helps the way they look, to themselves and to others. It also helps them win.

Before elaborating on the factors

affecting strength training, we want to set out here the *whys* of strength training for paddling. Is all this grunting necessary, when your style is so fluid already? Maybe when you're about to punt your last set of curls because you're really tired, the following will provide you the inspiration to gut it out.

All other things being equal (technique, endurance, mental aspects, equipment, luck, consistently blind gate judges, etc.), what advantages does the stronger paddler have over the weaker? In slalom, strength means quickness, cleanliness, and speed. (Hmmm, what else is there?) If you're stronger you can be quicker into eddies and out, quicker in spins, quicker to correct unanticipated boat movements, quicker to get back on line after (or as) a wave bounces you around. You will be cleaner, because you'll be more able to stop a drifting bow before it slides into a pole; you'll be able to complete a tough spin where the water gives you little help and a misplaced wave won't let you sneak. And you will be faster, because you won't drop low in eddies as you are able to translate downstream speed into upstream speed with pure brute strength. You will be backwards (and thus slower) less of the time because you can turn into reverse gates later and out of them sooner. You will gain valuable seconds because you can do a tough ferry right out of an upstream without going three boat lengths higher to catch the easy wave. You will be able to take the tightest, shortest line between all the gates. And if you are stronger, your muscles will last longer.

For wildwater, greater strength will do more than just move the boat farther with each stroke, though this is basically the fundamental goal. Strength will allow you to follow your line better, to be just enough more precise than your otherwise equal opponent who wanders a bit from his course and thus paddles a longer distance. Consider how close wildwater races can be: One fellow missed a place on the 1977 U.S. Wildwater K-1 Team by less than a second in 26 minutes *two days in a row.* An unbelievably strong performance came up short by a few feet over 5 miles, and he's still asking himself why.

Just to keep all of this in perspective, and lest you think strength training alone will make you a winner, we remind you of Bumbo. Bob (Bumbo) Robison was third in the 1979 World Championships in C-1 Slalom, and one look at him in a wet T-shirt will provide eternal hope for those of us who hate the weights, and want to rely on skill and technique.

Factors in Strength Training

The *mode,* or apparatus, is one of the least important variables. After pricing a complete Nautilus system, pick yourself up off the floor and remember 99.9% of the world's strength gain has been done without it! Homemade systems have created Olympic champions, and if you think you need fancy equipment, check out the forearm and hand strength in the next block mason you run into. A 110 lb. set of barbell weights with a set of dumbbells will cost only $20–30, and can be supplemented with a chin up bar to produce a very adequate weight set-up. Add more weight when you need it, and, by the way, be sure to use a spotter (friend who hovers over a weight that is threatening to drop on your neck) when you get into heavy bench presses or similar gaspers where dropping the weight could hurt. A lot.

Universal Gym equipment, designed for safety and convenience, and allowing many people to use the same equipment simultaneously, is probably the most widely used. You can change from 20 to 220 pounds on an exercise by moving a 6 ounce pin a few inches down the stack of weights—a lot easier than struggling with plates at the ends of a barbell. It's hard to beat the Universal for compactness and completeness in a standard exercise program.

Pulley weights, used primarily by swimmers because they can be made to simulate the actual strokes on dry land, allow paddlers to simulate their motions as well. One winter we worked together with pulley weights and found them to be a good complement to our Universal Gym workouts. A pulley weight workout is a two-step process. First, you sit facing the weights and *pull* as an imitation of the pulling part of the stroke. The next step is to sit facing away from the weights and imitate the *push* of the top hand. Twenty minutes of pushing and then 20 minutes of pulling will do the trick. In addition, a wide range of supplementary exercises can be done to augment the basic pushing-pulling movements.

Here is a good time to mention an important point to all the one-sided canoeists: Do all your strength training symmetrically, i.e. work left and right sides equally hard. You'll be glad you did as you develop and also when your career is over.

If you can secure access to a set

Barbells and dumbbells are the old standbys for strength training.

A Universal Gym will satisfy most paddlers' strength training needs.

of Nautilus equipment at a school or health club (or at a Nautilus Center, where the fee can be pretty substantial), by all means take advantage of it. Nautilus has the advantage of ease of change of the amount of resistance, like the Universal, but adds a new benefit: the machines are designed so that each exercise is done through the broadest range of motion possible, with the proper amount of resistance all the way through. Use of Nautilus machines allows a very specific, high-intensity workout that can really help your flexibility as well.

The optimum *rest interval* after a hard weight workout, before the next similar workout, is generally agreed to be 48 hours. In this case, optimum translates as minimum. Your muscles need that much time to recover, to take advantage by building back up stronger from the breaking down of tissue that occurred during the exercising. Not resting is as bad for you as not working hard during the session: both deprive you of maximum strength gain potential. Thus, three weight workouts a week is a good routine.

Wall pulley weights. Note the specialized bench with indentations for a paddler's feet.

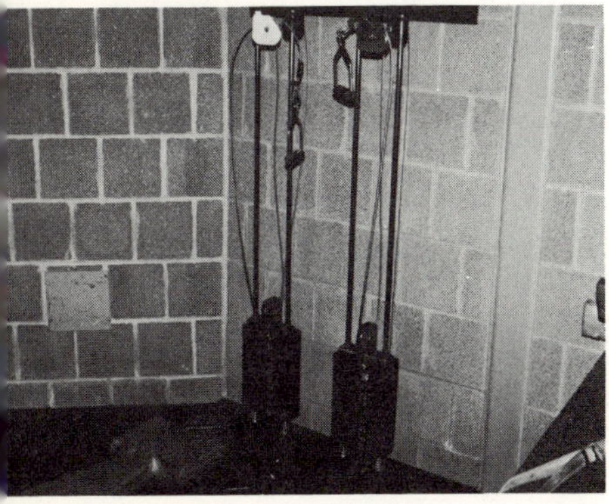

Duration: Most regular weight lifters, paddlers included, are guilty not of spending too little time on the weights, but of spending too much. That is, they do an exercise, fiddle around, talk about the weather, expound again on how they hate pull ups, etc., until five minutes have elapsed before the next effort. An hour and a half or two hours later they walk out of the weight room impressed with such a long session, ready to tell anyone who asks that they lift weights two hours a day, every other day. What a waste of time! For paddlers especially, who are concerned with only the upper part of the body in the first place, *no more* than an hour is needed to do a sufficient (in fact, optimal) number of sets of enough exercises. This all boils down to the one absolutely key, single, most important factor in strength training (may I have the envelope please?)—*Intensity.*

All the megabucks Nautilus equipment in the world isn't worth a damn just sitting there; barbells, pulleys, and stacks of Universal weights are extremely benign at rest. They can help you only if you really use them. A strength training session must be *intense* to be of value, and getting back to duration, if it is intense, it must be relatively brief—45 minutes to an hour for us paddlers. The body will not take any more; if it can, the intensity is not there. What does this mean? It means brief rests between sets, it means you should be breathing hard the whole time, and it means your pulse rate stays between 130 and 180 for the entire workout. Discussing last year's 29th place finish in the Nationals can wait till you're in the shower—it may not be 29th again if you really concentrate during your weight workouts.

The *internal structure* and order of a strength workout is the subject of ongoing debate. There are as many theories as there are trainers. Recognizing that the intensity of the session is crucial, there are many ways of going about it. Some say 3 sets of 6–8 repetitions with enough weight to make the last rep a real crusher, done in a "circuit" (i.e. with your 8 different exercises, you do one set of each, lower the weight in each a bit, then go back to a second set of each, lower the weights again, and do a third set) has been proven to produce optimum strength gain. Others, namely operators of commercial Nautilus Centers, which must survive financially and thus must break time-consuming bottlenecks on the apparati so the maximum number of people can get through, claim that each exercise should be done once only, with enough resistance (or weight) to allow 10–12 repetitions to the point of "momentary muscular failure." You really bomb an exercise, really do yourself in with one set, then move on to the next piece of equipment. One wonders whether the concept has been fostered by the commercial nature of the proponents, and the "proof" built to suit. (Regardless, you'll think you've been in a phone booth with an angry Apollo Creed after a Nautilus trainer runs you through one of these "character builders.") Basically, you should find what you like best, what produces the best results for you, and really work hard. If you stay at it for more than a couple of years, you'll eventually try all the theories yourself anyway.

The question of "high weight, low reps" versus "low weight, high reps" also has produced a bit of controversy and enough interested questions from paddlers to merit discussion. One theory states that heavy weights done only a few times create bulky power, but may not help flexibility or endurance, and that toward the racing season such training should gradually give way to lighter weights with many (20–50) repetitions. The same number of sets naturally takes longer to do, so it is less time-efficient, but proponents claim it is appropriate for endurance/strength training close to and during the racing season, after the heavy base has been built in the off season.

Another theory (which we happen to believe) says that not only is this program more time consuming, but it isn't doing what it says! The theory states that *muscular endurance* (as distinct from cardiovascular endurance), which is the ostensible goal of this shift in tactics to many repetitions, is in fact *directly* related to muscular strength, i.e., a muscle that can lift more weight on one repetition can do more repetitions at a lower weight—*because* it is stronger, it can last longer. You don't gain muscular endurance with more reps at lower weights, except that you are, almost in spite of yourself, adding muscular strength in the process.

Remember that we are not talking about cardiovascular (aerobic) endurance, which is related more to overall conditioning; we're talking about the ability of the muscle to perform repeated attempts at a given stressful task. Given that our strength training exercises are specific to paddling (i.e. the muscles worked help when we get in the boat), then this muscular endurance is indeed a desirable goal for both slalom and wildwater.

And where does this muscular endurance theory lead? It takes us back to muscular *strength* gain, as much and as efficiently as possible. Go for power, 3 sets of 6-8 reps, let the bulk come if it does, maintain flexibility with stretching and exercising through full range of motion, and do this all the way through the season! In the week or so before the big race you should back off a good bit to allow a complete recovery, and if you are racing many consecutive weekends use good sense: If you bomb yourself out three times a week on the weights you won't be worth much in your paddling workouts or in the race.

Realize that because so much other training is demanded of you during the season (stroke technique work, gates, intervals, etc.), your real strength gain will have to come before the season, while strength *maintenance* should be the goal during the season. You don't want to let yourself weaken as the big races approach. And precisely because you must do so much other work in the boat, you can't afford to do countless repetitions at low weights. Count on your paddling to build endurance of the whole paddling machine—you!

Specificity. The question here is whether paddlers should try to design strength exercises which exactly simulate various parts of the paddling motion, so as to build exactly and only the muscles that are needed. Many athletic trainers suggest that strength training should not be so specific, but should be used to increase strength of the relevant parts of the body generally. That is, for paddlers a program of upper body exercises aimed at all the relevant muscle groups makes more sense than trying to identify exactly how a certain exercise fits in to the stroke.

The key muscle groups for paddlers are stomach and back, shoulders, torso, biceps, triceps, forearms, wrists, and hands. Most of us do little leg work, and probably can do without a lot of neck bridging. The exercises suggested below attack all of these important muscles.

Programs

Having stated strongly that if the real effort is there in a workout, the method is of secondary importance, we'd like to present two possible programs, or series of exercises, that can serve as a starting point for your training program. First, a couple of pointers. If an exercise causes real sharp pain, don't fight it—stop. A wrist can sometimes get strained in trying to hold heavy weights for other muscles to work, and if you don't let it recover, you'll injure it further. Believe your body's signals (that doesn't mean quit because your body says "two sets is enough today, pal!").

Second, use a spotter on bench presses, otherwise you can't "max out" each set and really get the benefit of the last rep without risking your neck. Third, don't cheat. Curls are for your biceps, not to be heaved up with a dramatic hip thrust and back bend. Fourth, in general your breathing should conform to a simple phrase: blow the weight up. Breathe in as the weight comes down, breathe out as you push or pull or grunt to get it up. Don't hold your breath.

Program A—The Exercises. Equipment used: Barbells/Universal Gym and Dumbbells—(do three sets of each exercise)

Exercise	Repetitions	Weight as % of bodyweight
1. Sit-up	25–50	10 lbs (incline board)
2. Bench Press	10–12	80–120%
3. Bent Rowing	10–12	40–50%
4. Chin-up or Rope Climb	Maximum	
5. Back Hyper-extension	20	5–10 pounds
6. Curls	10–12	30–40%
7. Upright Rowing	10–12	30%
8. Pectoral Laterals	20	10% (dumbbells)
9. Back Laterals	20	10% (dumbbells)
10. Wrist Curls	50	10–30%

Description

1. Sit-ups can be done on the flat or on an incline board with a padded bar under which to tuck your feet. Bent-leg sit-ups tend to isolate the abdominals more than straight-leg sit-ups, and are thus better for paddlers. If you use a weight, hold it behind your head. Twist your trunk left, then right, then left, etc. on successive sit-ups.

2. The bench press works the entire pectoral (chest) area and, to a lesser extent, the deltoids (top of shoulder) and triceps (back of upper arm). Lie on a bench and start with the barbell at straight-arms length directly above the chest. A grip with hands spaced slightly wider than shoulder width is most often used. Lower the barbell straight down until it touches the mid-chest and press back to arm's length. Keep your butt on the bench, and use a spotter if you are working with a barbell rather than a Universal set-up.

3. Bent rowing exercises the lats (in your back) and biceps. With a slightly wider than shoulder width grip on the barbell, start bent over with torso parallel to the floor, legs slightly bent, and head supported. Pull the barbell up from the hanging position until it touches the mid-chest area and repeat. A good variation on this which relieves the strain on the lower back is "prone rowing," in which a sturdy narrow table 40″ off the floor is used. Lie on the table and lift the weight up to your chest the same as in bent rowing.

4. Chin-ups should be done with hands facing away from the body.

Be sure to go *all* the way down on each repetition. Rope climbing may be substituted for chins. We used rope climbing with great success one winter, doing them with the legs held straight out.

5. A back hyperextension is almost the opposite of a sit-up and isolates the lower back muscles. Universal Gym machines have a station for this or you can use a table with someone holding your legs. Lie face down on the table and slide off until only your legs are still in contact with the table. Begin with your upper body hanging straight down, then raise it as high as possible. Lower and repeat. For added resistance, hold a barbell plate behind your head.

6. Barbell curls are the basic bicep exercise (front of upper arm). Take a shoulder width undergrip and stand erect with the barbell across your thighs. Pin your elbows against your sides and move the bar with bicep strength from thigh to chin. No rocking or swinging is allowed. Curls can be done against a wall to ensure only the biceps are used.

7. The upright row is great for the arms and trapezius (upper back). Stand with feet apart and take a narrow grip (six inches apart) in the center of the bar with palms toward your body and the weight across your thighs. Pull the barbell upward close to the body until it reaches chin level. Emphasize a high elbow position at the top of the lift and then resist the weight on the way down.

8. Pectoral laterals isolate the pectoral muscles of the chest without involving the triceps. Lie on your back on a flat or inclined bench. Start by holding two light dumbbells at arm's length over your chest. Keeping your arms straight, lower the dumbbells out to the side, allowing them to descend as close to the floor as possible. Return to the starting position.

10. Wrist curls should be done near the end of each cycle of exercises, and should be done with both an underhand and overhand grip. Sit on a low bench with your forearms resting on your thighs. Bend the fists as far down as possible over the knee, even rolling the bar down your fingers. From this position curl the bar up as high as possible, flexing your wrists as hard as you can.

Program B

The weight used in the 3 sets should be 90%, then 85%, then 80% of the maximum with which you can do 8 repetitions.

1. Warm-up: stretching, 3 x 20 sit-ups, 3 x 25 push-ups.

2. Bench press—example: your 8 rep max is 100 lbs. Do your first set with 90, your second with 85, your third with 80. Do as many as you can in each set. As you get stronger, these training weights increase.

3. Upright rows

4. Wrist curls (be careful of popping something here with too much weight.) Do more reps with lighter bar if you have to; say 3 sets of 50 with 30 lbs.

5. Chin-ups

6. Bent rows

7. Pectoral laterals—dumbbells

8. Wrist rollers. A character

builder. Connect a 10 lb weight by a 6 foot rope to a dowel drilled so the rope wraps around the dowel as it rolls. Stand on a chair so with your arms extended straight from the shoulders (like you are sleep walking; you'll wish you were in a minute) the weight is off the floor. Roll the weight up to the dowel, then roll it down (don't zing it down, as in the Burton Method). Repeat till tears come to your eyes, arms straight out always. It won't take long. Work toward 3 sets of 5.

9. Curls

10. Punches—kayak sitting position, facing a window or mirror. With a 5 lb dumbbell in each hand, alternate horizontal punches straight out, elbows high (like a shot putter), big shoulder rotation. Do 3 sets of 100 reps.

11. French curls, for the triceps. Lie on your back with a light barbell on the floor above your head. Grasp the bar at shoulder width, palms up, elbows pointing at the ceiling. Now raise the bar to full arm extension without moving the upper arm. This can be hard on the elbows.

12. Dips. Super for shoulders and triceps. Gymnasts' parallel bars are great, but any similar station where you can support yourself with arms straight at your sides and feet off the floor will do. Jump up to the fully extended position, then lower yourself to where your upper arms are horizontal, then raise yourself back up.

13. Lateral raises, good for the deltoids on top of the shoulders. We have also called these "angel wings," remembering what it was like to lie in new snow and fan the arms out to leave the impression of an angel. Stand erect with a 5–8 pound dumbbell in each hand, and raise them to the side with arms straight, to a point just over head height. Lower and repeat.

14. Straight arm pullovers for chest and shoulders. On your back, grasp a barbell or weight plate on the floor with arms extended, palms up. Make a long arc over your head and down to your thighs, elbows extended throughout. Now arc back to the start.

15. Push-ups. A great warm-up calisthenic and a good shoulder exercise. Do them with hands spread to about paddle-grip width, and do them right: rise to full elbow extension, with head up and eyes straight ahead, then lower till you touch your chest, chin up. Keep a rigid body position. We've seen long necked ostriches who don't bend their necks as much as some expert push-up cheaters we know!

Building Stamina

During the off season when paddling is not possible, most serious paddlers engage in a cardiovascular sport to develop endurance or aerobic power. The best sports are running, cross-country skiiing, swimming, and wrestling. In fact, many of the best paddlers in the country have also been excellent cross-country skiers, including David Nutt, Doug Peterson, Brent Turner, Doug Armstrong, Chuck Lyda and Leslie Klein. The poling action necessary for cross-country skiing is very similar to the paddling motion.

Due to the recent findings at the University of Buffalo, running has come highly recommended as one of the best ways to develop endurance or aerobic power.

Being involved in a taxing, off-season sport is also mentally refreshing, especially if you are in a team or group. It's great to be around people who don't know a drawstroke from an eddy. It's also great for the mind to be bottom man on the totem pole in the new group and not worry about winning all the time.

Building Quickness and Agility

Many sports such as squash, tennis, handball, etc., are fine for improving hand-eye coordination, but are probably not as valuable for the paddler in the off-season as an endurance sport. Since aerobic power is so important, put your energies into developing that aspect of your repertoire and worry about developing quickness with on-the-water work.

Chuck Lyda skis cross-country during the winter to keep in shape. Photo by Bob Woodward.

Planning Your Year of Training

Equipped with the knowledge of different methods of training, both on and off the water, the next step is to ascertain when to concentrate on which aspect of training. Make sure that you are doing the right amount of the right kind of training at the right time of year. To help you put this puzzle together, we here present an overview of a year-round training plan. The following chart has as a target date August 15, the day of the biggest race of the year, the race of most importance to you in the entire season. Working backwards from that date, your plan should start with the months immediately following the last major race of the preceding season. A sample week from each time period is presented here as an example of what might be done in an average week during that particular training phase.

As with any detailed training program used as a model, treat this as such, adapting it to your specific needs. The chart outlines workouts for slalom and wildwater competitors. Of course, if you plan to do both, you'll have to modify your training to include the important aspects of each program. Wildwater competitors may also refer to the chapter on wildwater technique where a month-long daily schedule leading up to a major wildwater race is offered.

The term "general conditioning" refers to your overall fitness level, applicable to all sports. Specific conditioning refers to your fitness level related directly to paddling; i.e., those specific muscles used in paddling.

September–October–November

Emphasis

1. To relax mentally from the competitive season.
2. To increase level of general conditioning and improve aerobic power.
3. To improve weak technical areas.
4. To start involvement in an off-season sport.

	Wildwater	**Slalom**
Mon.	Weights	Weights
Tues.	Distance Paddling Running	Easy Gate Work Running
Wed.	Weights Running	Weights Running
Thurs.	Distance Paddling Running	Distance Paddling Running
Fri.	Weights Running	Weights
Sat.	Distance Paddling (or off)	Easy Gate Work (or off)
Sun.	Hiking, Running Race, Informal Whitewater Race	Easy Gate Work Running

December–January–February

Emphasis

1. To raise the level of general conditioning and aerobic power.
2. To begin specific conditioning.
3. Involvement in an off-season sport.
4. Technical work.
5. Indoor pool training where available.
6. For those in warm areas, continue to paddle 3–5 times/week, concentrating on developing aerobic power and, for slalom paddlers, gate technique.

	Wildwater	**Slalom**
Mon.	Weights Pool Training (Paddle Board)	Weights Pool Training (Gates)
Tues.	Off-Season Sport (or off)	Pool Training (Gates) Off-Season Sport (or off)
Wed.	Weights Off-Season Sport	Weights Off-Season Sport
Thurs.	Off-Season Sport Pool Training (Paddle Board)	Pool Training (Gates) Off-Season Sport
Fri.	Weights Off-Season Sport	Weights Off-Season Sport
Sat.	Off-Season Sport Pool Training (Paddle Board)	Off-Season Sport
Sun.	Off-Season Sport, Cross-Country Ski Race, etc.	Off-Season Sport, Cross-Country Ski Race, etc.

March–April

Emphasis

1. Obtaining feel again for the boat and whitewater.
2. Improve specific conditioning.
3. Early-season races.
4. Gradual changeover from dis-

tance paddling to faster forms of training.

5. Increase or maintain aerobic power.

	Wildwater	Slalom
Mon.	Weights Distance Paddling	Weights Fartlek Paddling Gate Work
Tues.	Fartlek Paddling Running	Gate Work Running
Wed.	Weights Distance Paddling	Weights Gate Work
Thurs.	Fartlek Paddling Running	Easy Intervals Running
Fri.	Weights Easy Intervals	Weights Gate Work
Sat.	Wildwater Race	Slalom Race
Sun.	Wildwater Race (or off)	Slalom Race (or off)

May–June

Emphasis

1. Improve specific conditioning.
2. Mid-season races.
3. Raise level of speed.

	Wildwater	Slalom
Mon.	Weights Distance Paddling Running	Weights Fartlek Paddling Running
Tues.	Intervals	Gate Work Intervals
Wed.	Weights Fartlek Paddling	Weights Gate Work Running
Thurs.	Intervals Running	Gate Work Intervals
Fri.	Weights Fartlek Paddling	Weights Sprint Paddling Easy Gate Work
Sat.	Wildwater Race	Slalom Race
Sun.	Wildwater Race (or off)	Slalom Race (or off)

July–Early August

Emphasis

1. Pointing toward big race.
2. Pure speed.
3. Specific conditioning.

	Wildwater	Slalom
Mon.	Weights Fartlek Paddling	Weights Gate Work
Tues.	Intervals Running	Gate Work Running
Wed.	Weights Sprint Paddling	Weights Gate Work Sprint Paddling
Thurs.	Sprint Paddling	Gate Work Intervals
Fri.	Running Easy Interval Paddling	Running Gate Work
Sat.	Wildwater Race	Slalom Race
Sun.	Wildwater Race	Slalom Race

Eric's Personal Notes With Regard to a Yearly Training Plan

In the 1979 season, leading up to the World Championships in early July in Jonquiere, Quebec, I altered my training schedule based on observations made during the physical testing program at the University of N.Y. at Buffalo and my own analysis of previous World Championships. In the past, my workouts in the early spring (March and April) consisted of hard interval workouts, both in the slalom gates and in a wildwater boat on flatwater. These workouts were carried into May and then on into the summer. With this program I reached a physical and emotional peak in late April and early May, a peak I was unable to hold or improve upon in June or July when the utmost in enthusiasm and strength was demanded. In fact, at previous World Championships I felt washed out, tired and mentally stale—not as strong or as eager as in April or May.

Therefore, that spring I held off doing anaerobic work until late May and June. I concentrated on aerobic work in March, April and early May, both in the gates and in the wildwater boat on flatwater. The result was that in the early spring I wasn't in peak form; I felt sluggish and slow in my movements both in practice and in races. My race results bore this out; I didn't win a race all spring and barely made the team in late May.

But late May was the time when I started doing intense intervals and hard gate work leading up to the July races at Jonquiere. During June, I could sense my improvement each week as my speed training sharpened the base which I had built in the early spring. The result was that in early July not only was I eager mentally, I was physically at a peak to race down the course.*

On the other hand, a paddler like Tom McGowan may have misjudged his spring/summer training program. Tom was hot at the Trials; he had been doing speedwork all spring. After the Trials, during June, he increased his work load, working out 2–3 times a day, with most of these workouts anaerobic. Allowing time to recover from a hard workout or having a rest day each week were ignored in favor of more and more work. At the World Championships he felt tired, both mentally and physically, and did not paddle up to his potential.

Wildwater kayak racers Dan Johnson and Bob Alexander are but two more examples of different approaches in training. Dan did not start his hard interval training until late in the season. In fact, he trained through all of the races leading up to the Trials in early June. If his schedule called for a workout the morning of a race, then the workout got the same attention as the race did that afternoon. When Dan finally started doing more speedwork and getting more rest before a race, he went on to win the Trials and do reasonably well at the World Championships.

Bob Alexander took a different course through the spring. He started his intervals in April and really pointed for many races during that month. Sure enough, Bob beat Dan in the early spring races, sometimes by over a minute. But whereas Dan improved and got faster all the way into June, Bob was unable to get much faster after May 1.

* My finish in the World Championships was not spectacular, but the blame cannot be placed on my physical preparation. My first run was one of the best I have ever had, but it was ruined by a bad decision at the bottom of the course. On the second run I was unable to regain the perfect intensity and focus I had on the first, so the overall result was disappointing.

Keeping a Training Log

The key to reaching your goals in whitewater competition, and the single most positive by-product of any athletic competition, is knowing yourself. "Know thyself" was a phrase coined by the ancient Greeks and it still holds true today.

The most effective way to monitor your progress is by keeping a training log. Each day you should record your workouts, rested pulse rate (taken in the morning prior to rising), weight, how you responded to the workouts, and general feelings regarding enthusiasm, overall fatigue, how much sleep you had, etc.

Accurate training logs can help you in planning future directions in training, tip you off if you're coming down with a cold and let you know whether you are overtraining. Reading back over your past workouts can also be a confidence booster when you're feeling low.

Overtraining

The never-ending problem in training is determining just how much training is optimum in order to reach your goals. Not enough training will leave you unprepared entering a competition. Yet, overtraining can be just as dangerous, if not more so. Signs of overtraining are lack of enthusiasm for training, chronic fatigue, sore joints and muscles day after day, a lack of improvement in workouts, and an abnormally high pulse rate.

A lot of the guesswork in training would be eliminated if we could just stick a finger into a computer and have it say, "Based on your present level of fitness, your workouts yesterday and the amount of sleep you had last night, you should do seven 60-second sprints with a 30-second rest this morning. This afternoon, three timed full-length runs should be sufficient."

Well, this computer hasn't arrived yet, although the East Germans are closer than anyone with their careful monitoring of their athletes. The DDR athletes are tested monthly in Leipzig and during training their blood lactate levels are measured daily to determine their level of fatigue.

We don't have access to such sophisticated measures, yet there is one way of determining your level of fatigue and this is through your daily pulse rate. After a month of monitoring your pulse at rest in the morning before rising, you'll have a pretty good idea of what it should be. Since the name of the game in training is stress followed by recovery, stress followed by recovery . . . you'll find that after a regular workout the pulse rate the following morning should be within a few beats of normal. A particularly hard training day may cause the pulse rate the next day to rise 5–8 beats a minute. This is an indication that your body has not recovered from the stress of the previous day and that you should take an easy day of training.

A rise in pulse rate may mean the onset of sickness, and the smart athlete will back off from training at the signs of a high pulse, sore throat and headache.

If you do get sick, knock off training altogether for a few days. Let your body battle the stress of the virus which is attacking rather than add even more stress by training too.

A wise old cross-country coach once said, "I would rather undertrain an athlete than overtrain him." Since some American paddlers are indeed overtrained, it is crucial to become aware of your body signals and take appropriate action before it's too late.

What happens if you find that you are overtrained? Take a few days off, get a change of scenery and do something completely different. Then come back and concentrate on distance work and gradually incorporate intervals back into your program.

Diet

One area of athletics which has drawn much attention in the past few years is diet. Despite this concern, there is still confusion and contradiction over what constitutes a "proper" or "balanced" diet for an athlete in training. It is not within the scope of this racing guide to present a complete discussion of diet. Those wishing to explore this subject in depth are requested to read *Food For Fitness,* published by World Publications, Box 366, Mountain View, California, 94942.

However, there are several observations which can be made here. Foremost, a diet sufficient in protein, carbohydrates, fats, vitamins and minerals—the traditional Middle American "balanced" plan of three square meals a day—will prove adequate for most people's needs. Secondly, with this typical diet, pay particular attention to avoid overeating. Moderation is the key word. Also, try replacing beef with fish or fowl and cut back on alcohol consumption. One or two beers at night, or some wine, will not affect your performance, however.

One topic under diet which has drawn considerable attention during the past few years is carbohydrate loading. A full discussion of this process will not be included here because it has been found that carbohydrate loading is of value only in events lasting more than an hour, such as a marathon running race. Since most wildwater races in this country are no more than 45 minutes in length this process will not be of value to wildwater paddlers.

Drugs

In our society, the word "drugs" has a negative connotation. Yet, some drugs are considered acceptable, such as aspirin, caffeine, medicines, etc., while other drugs such as heroin, LSD, cocaine, etc. are unlawful and considered dangerous. The line between these two types is very hazy and often defined by cultural norms.

The two drugs most often referred to in athletic circles are amphetamines (speed) and anabolic steroids. In all the years we've been involved in the sport, we've never seen an athlete using either of these drugs. In fact, we've never seen a performance so out of the ordinary that would suggest use by the performer. You do not need them, so do not fool with them.

Physical Problems

To most observers, whitewater racing seems like an exceedingly dangerous sport, with the risk of serious injury or even death ever-present. Actually, our experience and observations lead us to conclude that whitewater is in fact one of the safest sports around, though we have no desire to minimize the real risks. Cold water, a bang on the head, shortness of breath, and panic could combine to create a disaster anytime paddlers go out, so we must be careful never to let down our guard. Injuries of any kind, serious enough to halt training or racing, are indeed rare, and in fact neither of us has had such a problem in our combined careers of over 25 years of racing. The most serious, reasonably prevalent injury to paddlers is a shoulder dislocation, which unfortunately tends to recur about 75% of the time once a shoulder has been injured and the person continues paddling without corrective surgery. A few of our top paddlers—Bob Alexander, Dan Isbister, Carol Fisher, and Angus Morrison among them—have shoulder problems, but it seems they have had good success with surgery.

The best cure is to avoid the problem in the first place, which is partly a matter of good style, partly of luck. Avoid high or low braces with your arm being pulled up, out, and behind you, which is the vulnerable, "dislocate" position.

Paddlers who need glasses have a problem, because water splash, mist, and fog can really blur their vision and seeing reverse gates out of the corner of the eye can be tough.

If you normally wear glasses, try paddling without them to see if you can get along. If you are a true Mr. Magoo, consider using contact lenses. Many paddlers, Eric included, have used contacts with good success. Both hard and soft lenses are used, and we've heard few complaints about their falling out or being washed out by a splash of water in the face.

Cramped forearms can affect your paddle control, and are usually a result of gripping the paddle too hard. It is good to get used to relaxing your grip on the shaft during each stroke by releasing the grip of the last three fingers during recovery. Also, try a more oval shaft, which is easier to hold on to.

Strains and sprains of the forearm, wrist, and elbow are reasonably common, and unfortunately about the only remedy is rest. If you do strain one of these tendons, muscles, or joints, ease off a bit on the type of moves (strenuous Duffeks, for instance) that seem to place the most strain. Take a look at your paddling style and see if you can do differently the strokes that seem to be giving you the most physical problems.

6

Mental Preparation

While the physical aspects of successful training and racing have been given much attention in the relatively young history of whitewater sport, the more nebulous mental aspects of the sport have been neglected and misunderstood. Even now, our knowledge of the sports psyche is limited. Within this manual, physical preparation occupies well over twice as many pages as mental preparation, highlighting our lack of knowledge. This imbalance in knowledge is a result of several factors. One is that physical gains or losses are more easily measurable and noticeable. In many cases, simple tests will reveal progress or shortcomings. On the other hand, how does one gauge nervousness, experience or concentration?

A second reason is that physical ailments or problems are accepted topics of discussion in our society. Mental capabilities or weaknesses are seen in a dim light; it's an area we are reluctant to explore or discuss openly with others. It is easier and more acceptable to say that you were out of shape for a race than to admit that nerves caused you to perform poorly or that you could not push yourself any harder.

In Western society, we see mental forces such as fear, anxiety, lack of concentration, etc., as *inherent* weaknesses, weaknesses we have no control over and which we should keep to ourselves. Almost the opposite is true of physical problems, where we are only too willing to seek help for our ailments. *Sports Psyching,* by Thomas Tutko and Umberti Tosi (Hawthorn Books, 260 Madison Ave., N.Y., N.Y. 10016), presents a revealing discussion of the mental factors involved in sports. The book also offers specific exercises to help an athlete control tension and reduce fears.

The problem of dealing with the mental side of sports has been a great personal concern and interest. We have seen many more races lost due to poor mental "coping" than due to physical shortcomings. The single most serious mental problem we see is nervousness—fear of failure. When bothered by nerves before and during a race, the entire body becomes tight, and movements which were so easy in practice become exceedingly difficult.

A second major mental problem is a lack of concentration. Either by daydreaming, being distracted or showboating, racers hit slalom gates or lose their line in a wildwater race. We are speaking here from personal experience, and we are still searching for answers. In talking with other paddlers, we have found that these two major areas, tension and concentration, are of greatest concern. Hopefully, some of the things we have learned in dealing with these two problems will help you in resolving your own conflicts.

Tension

It's the day of the biggest race of the season. It could be the World Championships, the Nationals or a small, local race—its importance to you is all that matters. You've worked long and hard for this race—as long and as hard as anyone. You've planned, dreamed, made sacrifices, and this race is where all of the time and energy will bear fruit.

Yet, as you warm up in your boat prior to the start, you are almost overwhelmed by fear: the fear of losing, of doing poorly. In fact, if you could be anywhere else at that very moment, you would be. You just don't feel like your old self. The movements which were so easy the day before now seem forced and artificial. As you receive the final countdown, the tension is almost unbearable. When you start down the course, you're running on three cylinders; you're hesitant, jerky, and you feel tired much sooner than normal. You feel totally unequal to the task ahead. In short, you're not having any fun at all, which is the major purpose of racing, and you're certainly not doing your best.

Everyone has had similar feelings and has undergone embarrassing moments like this. Yet, some people seem to cope with the tension and perform well when it really counts while others never duplicate their training performances.

This problem should be approached in two ways. The first is to look closely at the fear of failure, and the second is to treat its symptoms.

Fear of failure cripples many athletes. They spend their time worrying about the final result (how they are going to do) rather than thinking about how to get the job done. You might as well face it, you're going to lose many more times than you're going to win. And as Rod Laver once said, "They don't shoot you when you lose."

During the first few years of his racing career, through about 1970, Eric was a wreck during the big races of the year. He would win every slalom race during the spring, and then David Nutt or someone else would beat him at the Nationals or the World Championships. In these big races, he underwent experiences much like those described at the beginning of this section. The overwhelming fear of losing dominated him.

In the past few years, he has taken a different approach to racing. He tells himself that he is going to do his best, and if he loses—then his hat is off to the winner. In other words, "I am going to go out there and lay one hell of a slalom run on these folks. If someone can beat it, then that person deserves to win."

Unknown situations or circumstances in which we are placed always raise our anxiety level (tension). Therefore, the situation of a big race (with lots of people looking on, the charged atmosphere, the expectations you and other people have, etc.) has to become routine: comfortable if possible. The physical procedure of running a 30 gate slalom course is easy to recreate and simulate and can be done every day if necessary. Yet, how do you duplicate the very special, once-in-a-year atmosphere of a big race and the internal pressures it creates?

Of course, one way to feel comfortable in big-race situations is to experience a lot of big races. The more you enter, the more relaxed and controlled you become. Another method is to go through the big race scene *in your mind* for a short period of time every day in the period leading up to the big race. Here's a process we have had success with:

1. Sit quietly with your eyes shut for about 15 minutes.

2. Try to envision yourself in the few minutes before the start of the big race. What do you see? What do you hear? What worries you? Try to generate all the fears/ tensions that you know will be with you at the start.

3. Next, say to yourself, "I recognize these fears, and I am not going to try and stop them. But, they are not going to prevent me from doing the task at hand. How I do it is more important than what happens after I do it."

4. Finally, envision all the possibilities that could happen on race day and how you will react if they should occur. Wind, low water, pouring rain, high gates, a superb first run by your competition, a lousy first run on your part, etc., should all be dealt with.

With this procedure, the unique circumstances of race day will be more familiar to you when the day arrives.

Concentration

We have always heard a person needed concentration to do well in slalom and wildwater racing, but nobody could define it or tell what it was like to concentrate properly. We still can't define it, but we know what it's like to have it and not have it. The best way to describe it is to imagine that you are going to be able to hear all of the following paddler's thoughts at a given moment during a slalom or wildwater race by tuning into his thought process. By breaking into this paddler's thoughts during a race, you can get a feel for what somebody might be telling himself as he negotiates one gate on the course with full concentration.

"Coming up to Gate 3, reverse. Have to turn at the last possible in-

---

1979 National K-1W Slalom Champion Linda Harrison, a superb example of the positive results of concentration and dedication. Photo by Barb McKee.

stant to save time. Keep to the right, though, because the water in the gate is moving toward the left pole. Watch the gate, watch the gate, watch the gate. Don't take my eyes off the pole. Turn now! Sink my stern under the red. Stay right, stay right! Draw on the right, draw, draw, draw. Counteract the water's force. Keep away from the green. O.K., body through the gate, sink the bow under the green. Throw my weight forward. Quick spin, quick spin, move, move, move . . ."

Of course, these thoughts are occurring in a split second. With full concentration on the task at hand, the finish of the run should see you mentally spent. An indication of less than total concentration would be thoughts such as "God, I've *got to have* a super run." "Isn't that George on the shore?—everyone must be watching!" "What if I don't make Gate 17?" "I've got a clean run going!" These thoughts indicate concern about how you are doing, what you look like on the course and your final placing, rather than focusing full attention to the actual "nuts and bolts" of the performance.

Concentration is just as important in wildwater as it is in slalom. Seemingly brief mental lapses bring on mistakes which cost time. Listen in on our wildwater racer as he negotiates a hard section of the course.

"Push, push, push. Get the most from each stroke. Where can I gain a second? Coming up to the big rock—want to be just outside the eddy line. Yes, right there. Stay there, stay there, stay there. Aim for the pillow to the right of the rock. *Not* here, straighten out, straighten out. Past the rock. On to the big waves. Stay left of center. Push, push, push . . ."

Doug Armstrong has said he was more tired mentally than he was physically at the end of the 1975 World Wildwater Championships after picking his way through a very technical and rocky course. The mental strain of being on the right line—that mysterious six-inch-wide ribbon of water which is the fastest in the river—is wearing.

During a wildwater race, there is more time for random thoughts to interrupt your concentration than in slalom. Examples: "Why am I so tired this early in the race?" "Who's in that car up on the road?" "If I don't have a good run through this rapid, there's no way I can win." "I wonder how Jim is doing?" These are all signs of a lack of attention to the task at hand.

Confidence

Is it possible to make a judgment whether top competitors are basically secure people, full of confidence, or basically insecure? We think not, largely because we have seen numerous examples of both personality types in the best racers, and we are not convinced that insecurity is a better motivator than self-confidence.

Some competitors are insecure, and this leads them to compete against others to reaffirm their personal worth. They feel a need to compete, to determine over and over that they are better than their challengers. This might well explain the behavior of numerous champions in many sports who have established their excellence (superiority?) over a number of years but who continue to race and to win.

We would like to think, however, that there are other motivating factors, other behavioral rewards, which influence both the perennial and the aspiring champion. These are the positive internal values of response to a challenge, the setting out and working for a worthwhile goal, the desire to excel in a field, the desire to get the most out of one's body, and the real joy of success. Fear of failure does not really enter into this picture until the paddler has set such a high standard for himself that anything less than a decisive win is a disappointment. If the disappointment is severe or destructive, then the values which are doing the motivating should be reweighted so that defeat can be accepted gracefully without lowering the desire to win.

Even with this bit of perspective, nothing will boost your confidence more than a win or two. Then you will see that winning is, indeed, possible and given the right circumstances, you can do it again. With confidence, you can do as Kipling recommends and, "Treat both impostors (winning and losing) the same." A loss won't ruin your life and a victory is only for the moment.

A person who has confidence in himself is a wise and wily competitor, indeed. This person may lose the early spring races because he is using them as a springboard to the more important summer races—and early season losses will run off him like water off a duck. A secure person will work on his weak points in training and not be concerned about winning the workout. Such a racer isn't easily upset by sudden changes on race day such as water level, wind and cold.

Psyched Out and Psyching Out

Being psyched out usually means being afraid. A person who is psyched out by Gate Three is actually afraid of doing poorly on it. In just about every case, more familiarity and experience with the situations which psyche you out (rough wildwater courses, upstream gates, etc.) and not worrying about the results of your actions will overcome your fears.

We have never tried deliberately to psyche out anyone and wouldn't know how to go about it. Your biggest worry should be yourself; you

Becky Judd doesn't let the logs at a pre-World Championship training session affect her. Photo by Doug Morriss.

will have enough trouble trying to control yourself without worrying about influencing someone else's actions. Trying to psyche someone out is a waste of time and will probably backfire.

Personalities We Have Known

We thought it would be worthwhile to analyze certain personality traits we have witnessed while training and competing. In this way we can see how people react to fear of failure, lack of confidence and poor concentration. The idea here is not to criticize others for the sake of criticism, but to learn from these people and experiences so that you can improve yourself and be aware of mental pitfalls so as to avoid them. Any similarity between the characters mentioned here and real people is intentional, and we hope they can laugh along. After all, if you can't laugh at yourself, who can you laugh at?

1. Mr. "I can't paddle fast on flat, easy, wildwater courses."

Mr. Flat believes he can only do well in wildwater racing when the race is contested on difficult rapids where big water experience, balance and water reading are just as important as hard paddling and good technique. On the flat stretches of a particular course, or on easy courses, he feels he has no chance to do well. People have told him that his stroke is poor, and he is constantly beaten in flatwater workouts. During the flat sections of a race, he says to himself, "Uh oh, another flat section. This is where I lose time. Feel how slowly I'm going. Feel how sluggish my boat is. My stroke is terrible. Whimper, whimper, whimper . . ." The fact that he doesn't have to concentrate on water reading as much during the flat sections gives him an opportunity to think about his aching body, his problems, etc.

Mr. Flat could probably be no slower than anyone else on the flat, but he thinks he is, and thereby places a limit on his capabilities. He also should realize that being beaten in flatwater sprints does not preclude him from winning wildwater races. Mr. Flat would be better off accepting the fact that flat stretches are a part of the game and that everyone feels slow and tired on these sections.

2. Mr. "I must win every workout."

Mr. Training Champ (TC) is a real tiger during practice, especially when others are working with him. He sees training as a test, and will put his all into winning every gate sequence, or every sprint. In fact, his day is ruined if someone beats him in a workout, and his mood broadcasts his daily performance. To ensure a workout win, Mr. TC likes to have all the odds in his favor and will work with others only on facets of paddling in which he is good. For sprints, he always lines up in the fastest water. For wildwater runs, he always starts last to have people to chase.

Mr. TC demonstrates a lack of confidence in himself, as he must constantly reassure himself with every workout. (Why wait until the weekend when you can get an ego boost every day?) You are only as strong as your weakest point, but Mr. TC never works on his weak points during practice because someone might beat him.

Mr. TC fails to realize that the purpose of a training session is to *improve* a particular aspect of paddling, not *demonstrate* your skill in that area. Mr. TC also runs the risk of losing his mental enthusiasm for the important races because there are only so many times you can "Put your number on" before your well of enthusiasm starts to dry up.

3. Ms. "Did you see the ridiculous place they put gate 17?"

Highly visible before a slalom event, Ms. Snit is always upset by the placement of one or more gates on the race course which she feels are positioned stupidly or unfairly. She dances a little jig in frustration on the bank in view of others analyzing the course. She might even proclaim loudly to those present that if the race committee persists in keeping the gate, then she will refuse to run it!

There's a bit of Ms. Snit in all of us, for we all need something to complain about. After all, if everything were perfect, the results would have been mailed to us prior to the race and our names (naturally) would be at the top of the list.

But extreme cases of Ms. Snit show a lack of confidence and a fear of failure. Her loud protestations over a gate give her an "out" in case she misses the gate (of course she missed it, it was stupidly positioned). In the back of her mind is the haunting fear that someone might be able to do the crazy gate and she won't.

On the other hand, beware the wily competitor who doesn't care where or how the gates are hung. He realizes that everybody has to run the same gates and feels that he can run them better than anyone else—no matter where they are. Little matter that the gate is set up on the road; he quietly prepares to get his boat up the bank in the shortest time possible!

4. Ms. "I haven't trained at all for this race."

Ms. Ill-Prepared bounces out of the car at the race site with this startling news. She is extremely anxious to tell everyone, particularly her competition, about her lack of preparation for this event. By doing so, she has given herself the perfect "out" in case she does lose.

If she wins, it must be because of her tremendous natural ability (after all, she won with no training!). If she loses, it's because she hasn't trained (of course, she told you so). Rare is the person who can say to himself, "I have trained as hard and as well as possible for this event. If I fail, it is because other people were better, and I am willing to live with the fact that I laid my best on the line and it wasn't enough. Period."

5. Mr. "The wind is blowing, therefore, I have no chance to win."

Mr. Outside Factors is using the elements as a crutch in case of failure. In other words, if he fails it is due to factors outside his control, such as wind, low hanging gates or a higher than normal water level. Mr. OF somehow thinks that these factors affect only him.

Yet, be danged if the wind doesn't blow for everybody, and it will blow a gate away from you just as many times as it will blow it into you for a penalty. Irregular outside factors add more variables to the game. The more variables, the more interesting the game, and the more you must fall back on talents you can't train for—resourcefulness, natural instincts.

Everyone has to face the outside factors, and if everyone is going to think of them as *disadvantages,* you might as well think of them as *advantages.*

7

Equipment

Endless arguments persist as to the merits of different types of equipment for paddling; we all know the "equipment freak" who spends an impossible amount of time thinking, talking and expounding about what equipment is best, and why. Compared to most other sports, it is difficult to spend tons of money on paddling gear—you would be hard pressed to spend $1,000 on a complete set of the fanciest gear available. You might well find yourself competing against the fellow who has spent $200 total to outfit himself with a lighter boat, as good a paddle, and the bare necessities. Remember, necessities, by definition, are all that are needed to win.

Before we dive in to this discussion, be aware of two things. Much highly technical analysis of each piece of essential racing gear has already been done, most notably in a series of evaluative articles in *Canoe* Magazine (kayak paddles, helmets, life jackets). A list of these articles appears at the end of this book. It is not our purpose here to delve so deeply, but rather to give you the tools with which to make your decisions about what you need. Second, you must be happy with the equipment you have for a particular race, and make it work for you, rather than against you. In other words, you must *control* your boat, paddle, skirt, clothing, etc. to the extent it is in perfectly adequate shape, and then you must cease to worry about it, or cease longing for something better. Our advice is for you to take a *utilitarian* approach to your equipment, so it is perceived as a set of tools, rather than a set of toys. Tools are used to do a job, to accomplish a purpose, and yet can be exquisite in design, shape, and their functional nature. Toys are made to be played with, to distract and to entertain (and, it seems at Christmas, to break). Tools are a means, toys are an end. Your racing equipment should be the former. After all, 80% of the perfect finish on a $400 boat will get scarred within a week so why pay $400 in the first place? $100 is for the finish!

We have often seen paddlers win in 35-pound tubs or with a patched, heavy cruising paddle. It's tougher to do that these days, because so many of the top competitors have the best available equipment. If you plan to compete at a high level, you must not allow yourself to be at a disadvantage with your equipment—a heavy, obsolete boat, a slalom paddle in a wildwater race, etc. However, until you approach the top level, try to avoid becoming preoccupied with boat designs and all manner of "ultra" equipment. It is not necessary, and in fact is dangerous: it can distract you from the more important factors determining your immediate success and how fast you improve. Those are your technique, fitness and experience. Somewhere along the line you will want to "trade up," but don't spend money just for the sake of looking hot and nasty. The old saying from the world of auto racing fits well here: "If it don't go fast, chrome it!"

Forewarned, read on. What follows is a brief description of equipment evolution over the brief history of our sport, then a quick look at the major items you need for racing, boats and paddles, and what to look for. We conclude with a rundown of some accessory gear: helmets, life jackets, spray skirts, wetsuits, shoes, pogies, paddle jackets, grunch pads, and ways of waterproofing your boat.

Boats

History

Since international slalom racing originated in 1949, boats have done two things: become rigid, and shrunk, both in size and weight. Kayak racing was initially contested in both F-1 and R-1 classes, meaning folding and rigid construction, while the first racing canoes were open boats with canvas decks stretched across the gunwales. Additionally, until the major rules changes in 1971 and 1973, race boats could have no concave cross-sectional surface curves, and canoes were forced at least to give a nod to the shape of the traditional Canadian canoe, with the ends higher than the middle. Finally, the minimum width on C-1's was reduced from 80cm to 70cm. Now, all slalom boats need meet only minimum length and width requirements, and wildwater boats have a minimum width and maximum length.

This reduction of the rules to the most simple dimensions has fostered a succession of slalom boat design changes, leading to boats of small size and weight that would have been undreamed of 15 years ago. Kayaks must be 4 meters long and 60 cm wide, and a modern race boat now weighs 15–18 pounds and requires the paddler to grease up before trying to slide in. We are approaching limits imposed by the quite unavoidable need for the kayaker to have his feet in front of him and still in the boat. Yet, even that may vanish: the always innovative (not to say bizarre) French raced a C-2 several years ago with *no* cockpits, no openings *through* the deck, but, rather, depressions molded to the shape of the paddlers' lower legs bent back in the kneeling position. The boat was nowhere more than 6″ deep, but for some reason was confined to the scrap heap—we believe they kept falling off of it (notice we did not say out of it). Watch for this concept to return legitimately. It already is used successfully in "surf-skis," where the surf-paddler sits on his "boardyak" and pushes against raised footrests for attachment to the craft.

With absolutely no limitations on design of boats, slalom kayaks, C-1's and C-2's are approaching minimum volumes. They turn well, track well and contain so little buoyancy they can be slipped under poles with a slight forward or backward lean into or out of a gate. Slalom technique thus now requires incredible quickness, as the paddlers, in order to be competitive, must take advantage of the ability of the boats to minimize the time spent sideways to the current in spin moves and the time spent in upstream gates. This has fostered a move to shorter paddles, because so much intricate maneuvering takes place in the gate (where extra lumber only gets in the way).

The latest rule change, effective January 1, 1979, orders race organizers to hang the poles no closer than 10 centimeters (approximately 4 inches) to the water, whereas before it was mandatory the poles be set as close to the water as possible while remaining still. This should decrease the time spent getting through upstreams since low-volume boats will no longer need to be put "through" in the conventional sense, but simply under a pole going in and under a pole going out. It will push us further toward the minimum 90° turn needed to slide under both poles in a reverse gate. Gate judges must be situated on the gate line to make sure turns are completed! This means low volume will continue to be the rage, since the lower the volume, the less worry of hitting the poles. What it means for you is, in your training and racing, *after* you have learned the fundamentals of going through the gates "properly" (i.e. the "old" way), you will have to learn how, and equally as important, when, to sneak. As you improve and try to be competitive with the top guys, you will have no choice but to get yourself a "sneaky" boat for racing. Because this boat is not particularly comfortable and must be very light to be competitive, you will also have to have at least one other boat for cruising. If you train for slalom in rocky or big water, you will probably also need a low-volume training boat as well, because your race boat probably won't be able to withstand the abuse.

Our advice: if you plan to compete in the slalom Nationals, you need a light, low-volume race boat of a currently popular design. Buy it or build it, make sure it doesn't leak and become comfortable with its handling characteristics.

Wildwater canoes and kayaks have always been a compromise between a boat which is extremely fast on flat water and one which is very stable and comfortable to paddle in big water.

The fast flatwater design will be unstable and will usually have a long, narrow bow which will tend to bury itself in standing waves, thereby reducing your forward

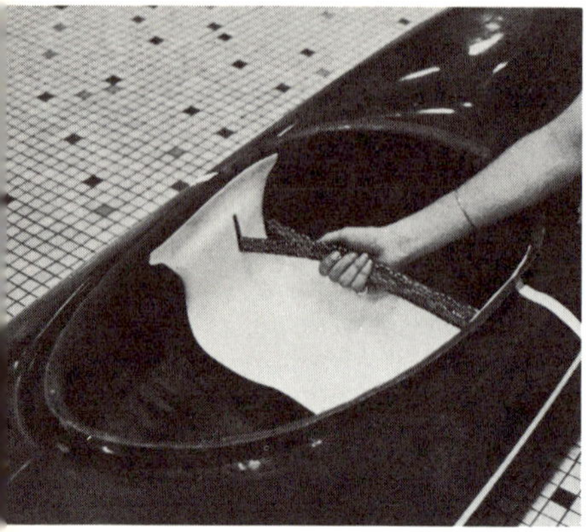

A simple backstrap.

A fully equipped seat area.

speed. The instability of the boat will necessitate bracing strokes and energy in order to keep it upright in turbulent situations.

The slower (on flatwater), more stable design will usually have additional volume in the bow which will resist submersion. However, this same boat will be slower on the flat and easy-water sections of the race course.

With this in mind you can pick a design best suited for the wildwater races you plan to enter. If most of your racing is going to be done on easy courses such as the Nantahala or the Red Moshannon, then your boat should have more flatwater design characteristics.

If, on the other hand, you plan to race at Buena Vista or on the Savage, then a boat with a full bow and adequate stability is a must.

Remember, it isn't always a case of being skilled enough to make a fast, flatwater design work for you in big water. There are times when these designs are inappropriate, and no amount of practice, balance or training will overcome these design deficiencies.

Paddles

As was mentioned previously in this chapter, the trend to shorter slalom paddles makes sense, and beyond recognizing that, you need only buy one you like. We prefer, and have always used, wooden paddles, but there are many excellent synthetic paddles as well. Few slalom kayakers are using paddles as long as 210 cm. now; many use a 208 cm. length or less. Most slalom canoeists are in the 52–58″ range. For any paddle, an oval shaft is helpful to give you a feel for blade angle, and a metal tip can help in rocky streams.

Kayakers might consider blades offset less than 90 degrees, which require less stress on the control wrist and allow subtle advantages in speed.

Wildwater kayak paddles are mostly in the 214–218 cm. range, although some paddlers prefer shorter paddles for big-water races. These paddles have slanted tips for a smooth entry into the water and are lighter than slalom paddles simply because they do not need to be as stout. Wildwater canoe paddles are usually 1–3 inches longer for the same person than the slalom paddle, for better reach, to compensate for the higher seat in the wildwater boat, and because there are no gates to hit! These, too, should be lighter than their slalom counterparts, and should *not* have metal tips on them, which are unnecessary and can only cause problems. In the 1976 Savage International, Gordon Grant, John's C-2 partner, had his metal-tipped paddle ripped from his hands as it caught on a rock. The paddle floated free, but it took John and Gordon at least 20 seconds to slow the boat down enough to retrieve the paddle—they finished fifth, 24 seconds behind the winners.

Because a canoe stroke rarely begins with the tip of the blade absolutely square to the water, there is a slight torque put on the paddler's hands each time the inside corner of the blade catches before the outside corner. Paddle makers have copied the kayak blades and slanted the tip, to reduce the fatiguing torque by causing the tip to enter smoothly and all at once.

Our experience has been that this problem is largely mythical, and that any narrow, light blade works well. Of course, switchers cannot make use of the slant-tip blades. It is probably a good idea to have a special wildwater paddle that is light, has a thinner blade, and is a few inches longer than your slalom paddle, but don't be distressed if it does not have a slanted tip.

Lifejackets

The two essential pieces of safety gear for whitewater paddling are a lifejacket or PFD (Personal flotation device) and helmet. Both are required on any race course. Modern PFDs are so light, comfortable and form fitting that there is no reason not to wear one, and all leading whitewater paddlers and racers do. ICF rules require a buoyancy of six kilograms (approximately 15 pounds), which is enough to be a great help to a tired paddler who has just missed three roll attempts and must swim. Most U.S. Coast Guard approved type III vests will pass any test the ICF may require. We recommend that you buy only a Coast-Guard approved vest, and that you wear it in whitewater at all times and even during practice on flat water in order to become familar with it.

At the 1979 World Whitewater Championships in Jonquiere, Quebec, Harishok introduced a spraycover-lifejacket combination for kayakers with the buoyancy located in the front part of the garment. As the kayaker sat in his boat, the bulky buoyancy was situated over his knees and upper thighs. This left the upper torso free of material and thus cut down on bulk which might hit a slalom pole and/or restrict his movements.

Many paddlers tried it and liked it and it only remains to be seen whether it will become standard equipment in the future. However, a beginning racer would be better off with a traditional vest and then move up to this new "combo" when skill level demands the ultimate in equipment refinement.

Helmets

Since you will try to stay in your boat and roll up if you capsize, you must wear adequate head gear. Many racers wear very light plastic shells with a skimpy suspension system inside which are not bombproof; others wear tougher, motorcycle-type helmets which give better protection but are heavier. Our advice is to opt for lots of protection until you have been around long enough to make a different decision based on your own wisdom and experience. You may change helmet styles, you may not. In any case, always wear a helmet in whitewater! (We find them most useful against the heavy slalom poles in use these days.) As with a PFD, wear it during practice to become used to it, even if you practice on flatwater.

Spraycovers

A good spraycover is an obvious necessity, but you would be surprised at how many good racers allow theirs to deteriorate alarmingly before replacing them. The skirt must be watertight both top and bottom and must be tested on the race boat before the race to make sure it will stay on; it is stupid to use a new spraycover for the first time on race day, since if it blows off you'll have wasted a run. If it is a wildwater race, you'll have wasted an entire weekend.

Neoprene has proven to be the most popular and watertight material available for spraycovers. Most racers use an all-neoprene or nylon-top neoprene-bottom combination. You can make your own with a square yard of ⅛″ thick neoprene, a few feet of shock cord, a small can of neoprene glue and small amount of toluene to clean the surfaces before gluing.

Beware of making your spraycover too tight around the upper waist in the interest of keeping water out. If it's too tight it will cramp your breathing and your paddle movements.

Combatting the Cold

Combatting cold weather and water means retaining body heat, which is best accomplished with a wet suit, a wool sweater and hat, a paddle jacket and pogies. Combinations of all of these can be used to make racing and training reasonably comfortable down into sub-zero temperatures, and often are used even on hot days if the water is very cold. Kayakers can wear a full-length Farmer John wetsuit, while the kneeling canoeists usually must use a shortie or cut out the backs of the knees of the Farmer John to allow circulation to the feet. During a race, a wetsuit is rarely worn due to its restriction of movement.

Wetsuit booties are a wonderful invention, and while wetsuit gloves and mittens are very warm, they limit the feel for the paddle shaft needed for precise control and can be very tiring. A marvelous recent invention known as the pogie keeps the hand adequately warm, weighs almost nothing, and allows normal paddle control, since it is simply an elongated sleeve that encases the hand after it has grasped the paddle shaft. Pogies are a God-send for winter training.

Finally, a good nylon paddle jacket, worn over a wool sweater if necessary, completes your paddling wardrobe, providing protection from the elements and infinite possibilities for gaudy displays of color and design. Elastic at the waist and velcro or elastic at the wrists and neck should keep most of your body heat in, keeping you warm in mildly unpleasant weather that is not severe enough to require a wetsuit.

Boat Flotation

ICF rules indicate that you must render your boat unsinkable and require that you have some kind of adequate flotation in both bow and stern. Most racers use ethofoam walls in bow and stern to satisfy this rule. Keep in mind that while this satisfies the rule, ethofoam walls are generally not adequate in keeping your boat on top of the water after a capsize. For whitewater practice, we recommend additional float bags which can be secured alongside the walls.

Equipment Measuring

At National Championships or international events, expect to have all of your equipment measured and tested to see whether it conforms to ICF regulations. At local or regional races, this will not be required. If you go to a race which will have equipment measuring, it's a good idea to check your equipment beforehand *and*

A paddler slips into Pogies.

take appropriate materials to the race for repair in the event your equipment proves inadequate.

Waterproofing Your Boat

Having water in your boat during racing or training is an obvious disadvantage. Here are some tips in keeping water out:

1. A recessed cockpit rim is better than a rim raised above the level of the deck. The former will avoid a direct hit of water which can drive up underneath a spraycover and into the boat.

2. Another method of avoiding water being driven up underneath a spraycover is to employ a spray shield. After putting your spraycover on, tape a plastic garbage can liner over the deck and the front and sides of the spraycover.

3. Waxing your entire boat will be a very temporary solution to pin holes in your fiberglass boat. However, it will keep some water out for the length of a race.

4. Wildwater paddlers often practice with "Grunch Pads" on their bow and sterns. By using wax paper and/or wax and releasing agent, mold additional fiberglass shields over the places which take the most abuse. After separating the new pad from the boat, it can be taped on for the next practice run. After practice, remove the pad just before the race and your original hull will be smooth and crack-free.

A recessed cockpit, on the near kayak, is better than an elevated cockpit for keeping out water. Photo by Bob Woodward.

A plastic garbage bag taped over the front of the spraycover will help waterproof the boat. Photo by Bob Woodward.

A thin sliver of neoprene under the lip of the combing will help keep water out.

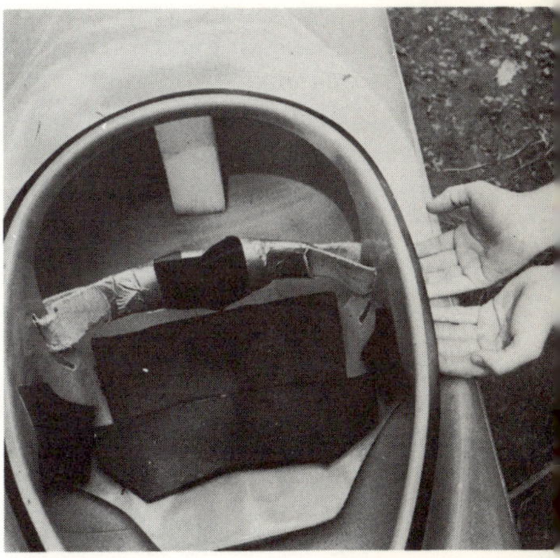

8

Commonly Asked Questions

Q. Who conducts whitewater events in this country and what procedures do I follow in entering a competition?

A: The American Canoe Association (ACA) is the oldest national canoeing organization and is the official spokesman for all canoe racing activities by way of affiliation with the International Canoe Federation. Slalom and wildwater racing is governed by the National Slalom and Wildwater Committee of the ACA which is responsible for all rules pertaining to racing as well as for the sanctioning of all races held in this country.

Membership in the ACA is required for participation in National and Divisional championships and the annual dues in 1980 were $20. The address of the ACA is P.O. Box 248, Lorton, Va. 22079. We recommend joining the ACA, not only to be able to participate in national events, but also to support the many programs in other canoe-related fields where the ACA is active.

The NSWC's duties also include publishing a monthly newsletter (which we recommend highly as a source of information), a yearly schedule of races (listed in the newsletter) and conducting a yearly ranking system of whitewater racers within their respective classes. In order to be eligible for ranking, and to receive a race schedule and monthly newsletter, we also encourage you to join the NSWC for $6.50 (1980 dues). The Chairman of the NSWC is Steve Parsons, 2878 Holmes Ave., Minneapolis, Minn. 55408.

The ACA and the NSWC consist of volunteer paddlers working to help the sport of canoeing. In addition, volunteers organize the almost 200 whitewater races held each year. To enter a race, write the race director well in advance (race director's names will be listed in the schedule) and ask for an entry form and send a stamped, self-addressed envelope.

The yearly ranking classifies competitors in A, B, C or D categories depending on their results from the previous year. Some races are open only to boaters within a certain classification, and this restriction will be listed on the race schedule. While some races have an entry deadline in advance of the race, other races will allow you to enter at the race site on the morning of the race. In any case, it is well-advised to check ahead of time with the race organizer.

Entry fees usually range from $3–$7 per person per event.

Q: Should I specialize in either slalom or wildwater?

A: There are notable exceptions to every rule (Cathy Hearn in 1979 is one example), but by and large the days of doing well in both disciplines on the national, and especially the international, level are over. If you want to reach the top against today's competition, you must put all your energies into one area. However, if your goals are on the local level, we feel there's no harm in doing both.

In addition, beginners of all ages, and young junior paddlers, should at least practice and race in both areas in order to experience all that the sport has to offer.

Q: What techniques do you employ in memorizing a slalom course?

A: Course memorization becomes easier with experience. We recommend drawing a course map the night before the race and studying it at dinner or before you go to bed. Then, break the course down into manageable sections of five gates each and memorize one five-gate section before moving on to the next.

One mistake many whitewater slalomists make is looking at a slalom course from only one bank. Analyzing a course from both sides of the river and from all possible angles is crucial, even if it means getting in your boat and paddling over to the other side on a cold, wet race morning.

9

Reference Sources

Magazine Articles available from

Canoe, 131 E. Murray St., Fort Wayne, Ind. 46803

Past copies available for $2.50.

1. "How to Buy a Wet Suit" March/April '74
2. "How to Pick a Paddle" March/April '75
3. "How to Set Up a Slalom Course" March/April '75
4. "Whitewater Helmet Evaluation" Nov./Dec. '75
5. "Type III Life Jacket Evaluation" July/Aug. '76
6. "Whitewater Kayak Paddle Evaluation" March/April '77
7. Accessories Guide Nov./Dec. '77

Diet

1. *Food For Fitness,* World Publications, Box 366, Mountain View, Calif. 94040.
2. *Let's Eat Right To Keep Fit* by Adelle Davis, New American Library, 1301 Avenue of the Americas, New York, N.Y. 10019.

Strength Training

1. *The Complete Weight Training Book,* by Bill Reynolds, World Publications, Box 366, Mountain View, Calif. 94040.
2. *Strength Training Principles,* by Ellington Darden, Anna Publishing, Inc., 500 St. Andrews Blvd., Winter Park, Fla. 32792.

Aerobic Fitness

1. *The Complete Runner,* World Publications, Box 366, Mountain View, Calif. 94040.
2. *The Complete Woman Runner,* World Publications, Box 366, Mountain View, Calif. 94040.

Mental

1. *Sports Psyching,* by Thomas Tutko and Umberto Tosi, J. P. Tarcher, 9110 Sunset Blvd., Los Angeles, Calif. 90069.

General Boating

1. *Kayaking,* by Robert J. Evans and Robert Anderson, Stephen Greene Press, Brattleboro, Vt. 05301.
2. *Boat Builders Manual,* by Charles Walbridge and Steve Rock, 230 Penllyn Pike, Penllyn, Pa. 19422.
3. The American Canoe Association, P.O. Box 248, Lorton, Va. 22079.
4. The National Slalom and Wildwater Committee of the ACA, 2878 Holmes Ave., Minneapolis, Minn. 55408.